Dear Ms. Handelman,

I enjoyed your cla

a very good philosophy teacher. However, I realized that life can b̶ not be fully explained by human philosophy. The truth is not in our mind, but in our spirit. Anyway, I don't want to force you to believe what I believe. I hope you would like to read this book. Religion is different from Christ, who is the real God, and who is the truth. I hope you will find the truth.

Vivian
May 19, 2000

LIVING STREAM MINISTRY

CHRIST *versus* RELIGION

WITNESS LEE

Anaheim, California • www.lsm.org

© 1971 Living Stream Ministry

First Edition, July 1971.

ISBN 0-87083-010-4

Published by

Living Stream Ministry
2431 W. La Palma Ave., Anaheim, CA 92801 U.S.A.
P. O. Box 2121, Anaheim, CA 92814 U.S.A.

Printed in the United States of America

99 00 01 02 03 04 / 17 16 15 14 13 12 11 10 9 8 7 6 5

CONTENTS

PREFACE

This book is composed of messages given by Brother Witness Lee in Los Angeles, California in July 1970.

CHAPTER ONE

CHRIST THE BRIDEGROOM

Scripture Reading: Matt. 9:14-15; Luke 5:29-30, 33-35

From the record of Matthew we see that all things related to Christ took place outside of religion. In that day, Judaism was the genuine religion, the religion founded according to God's Holy Word. But everything concerning Christ took place outside of that. In other words, Christ had nothing to do with religion.

CHRIST'S BIRTH OUTSIDE OF RELIGION

The record of Matthew chapter 1 tells how the birth of Christ was accomplished outside of Jerusalem, away from the temple, having nothing to do with the holy priests. God did not send the angel Gabriel to the family of the priests; God did not send Gabriel to someone praying in the temple in Jerusalem. God sent His angel to a little town in a despised country, Nazareth of Galilee. He sent him to a girl, a virgin, in a poor family. Practically everything related to this girl and her situation was outside of Jerusalem, the temple, the holy priesthood, the typical and genuine religion. The birth of Christ has nothing to do with religion; it is absolutely accomplished outside of religion.

You may say that Jesus was conceived in Nazareth, but born in Bethlehem. But if we look into the record carefully with the light of the Holy Spirit, we see that this was accomplished in a hidden way. We may even say that He was born there "sneakily," just to fulfill the prophecy. He was suddenly brought to Bethlehem to be born, and then, just as suddenly, He was brought away.

The birth of Christ has nothing to do with anything religious.

CHRIST FOUND OUTSIDE OF RELIGION

Matthew chapter 2 then proceeds to tell us how people found this Christ. He was not found in religion, neither was He found by any religious people. He was not found in Jerusalem, He was not found in the temple, neither was He found by any priest or any holy people. We are all familiar with the account of the heavenly star appearing in a pagan country to people with no Bible and no genuine religion. We know also how those heathen wise men exercised their natural mind, concluding that the King of the Jews should be born in Jerusalem. In so doing, they caused many young lives to be taken. But eventually they found Jesus. They found Him mainly not according to Biblical knowledge. You remember that when they came to Jerusalem, King Herod called the scribes and the Pharisees, those who had the knowledge of the Bible. They all gave Herod the proper and exact quotation, Micah chapter 5, verse 2, telling that Christ would be born in Bethlehem. They had the knowledge, they had the exact scriptural references, but none of them went to see Christ. They were for the Scriptures, they were for the Bible, but they were not for Christ. They paid attention to Micah 5:2, foretelling the coming of Christ and even the birthplace of Christ; yet, when the news came of Christ's birth, none of them went to behold it. The Christian religion today is exactly the same in principle. People talk about the Bible and have the knowledge concerning Christ, but rarely do you find one who really cares for Christ. They care for the Bible, they care for the prophecies, but they do not care for Christ.

Praise the Lord, there were some pagans from a pagan land who did care for Christ. The record of Matthew tells us that after they departed from Jerusalem, the star appeared to them again. I tell you, when you leave the denominations, when you leave the Christian religion, the star is there. Hallelujah, the star is there! When you get into religion, you miss the star, you miss the mark. When you go to the religious people, when you attempt to follow the dead letter of the Scripture, you miss the heavenly star and can never find Christ. When the wise men departed from Jerusalem, lo, the star appeared. Hallelujah! How good it is to have a heavenly star! Then they found Jesus. The finding of Jesus is absolutely outside of religion.

CHRIST INTRODUCED OUTSIDE OF RELIGION

Matthew chapter 3 relates to us the principle of the introducing of Christ—this also is absolutely outside of religion. John the Baptist was the one who recommended Christ to the people. He was born a priest, but he would not remain in the priesthood, he would not stay in the temple or even in the city of Jerusalem. We read that he was in the wilderness. He stayed in a wild place, and even he himself became wild. He wore camel's hair. The camel, according to Leviticus chapter 11, was an unclean animal. But John said in effect, "You say, according to your religious regulation, that the camel is unclean. Then I must be such a camel!" What would you say? John acted in a way radically opposed to religion. And consider his diet. He ate wild honey and locusts. He had no religion, and he had no culture; he was versus religion, and he was versus human culture. He was not in the temple. He had no altar to offer sacrifices, he had nothing related to religion or even to human culture.

Not long ago in Los Angeles a brother came to the meetings wearing a blanket. This blanket was a real test to some of the people. But John the Baptist wore camel's hair. The blanket was cultured, treated, and made with human hands, but the camel's hair worn by John the Baptist was absolutely raw. He was wild; he was really wild. This was the pioneer, the forerunner of Christ. It was he who stood there and, seeing Christ coming, exclaimed to the people, "Behold, the Lamb of God." It was he who said that he saw the Spirit as a dove descending from heaven upon Christ, and he knew that

it was He who would baptize in the Holy Spirit. What
can we say? He said nothing about the ten commandments.
He gave that up. He said, "Behold the Lamb of God." He
pointed to the One who would baptize in the Holy Spirit,
and he said, "Repent!" John did not teach people about
religion—he called on them to repent, to change their
mind, to change their concept about religion and culture.
He did not tell them to do something, he baptized them,
he buried them, he terminated them. John said, "I baptize
you in water, but He that comes after me will baptize you
in the Holy Spirit."

What would you say? Jesus was recommended in such
a wild way. Would you believe? Would you take it? He was
recommended by a wild person in a wild way with nothing
to do with religion. Hallelujah for John the Baptist! He
was really good.

CHRIST FOLLOWED
OUTSIDE OF RELIGION

Matthew 4 tells us that after Jesus was introduced,
there were some dear ones who followed Him. Who were
they? The high priests? The scribes? No. They were the
Galilean fishermen. Some were fishing in the sea, others
were mending their nets—they were unlearned people,
but they followed Jesus. And they began to follow not in
Jerusalem, not in the temple, and not even in the Holy
Land, but in Galilee, a place then considered as "of the
Gentiles" (Matt. 4: 15).

You see, the birth of Christ, the finding of Christ, the
introducing of Christ, and the following of Christ were
entirely apart from religion. Then, Hallelujah, Jesus came:
He not only came in His birth, but He also came of age;
He came forth to minister, He presented Himself to the
people. He was there; He came to the people; there was
no need to go and find Him.

JOHN'S DISCIPLES BECOME RELIGIOUS

Skipping over Matthew chapters 5, 6, 7 and 8, we come
to chapter 9, where something very interesting occurred

(vv. 14-15). The disciples of John came to Jesus, talking about something religious. Could you believe that after such a short time the disciples of John the Baptist, who had nothing to do with religion, could fall into a kind of religion? They founded a new religion, and they took the lead to put a question mark upon the Lord Jesus. Furthermore, the disciples of John came with the disciples of the Pharisees (Luke 5:30, 33). What company! The Pharisees were the old-timers of religion. The disciples of John were the new-timers; they had only been on the way for perhaps two years. Yet within such a brief period, the disciples of John had become religious.

"Then came to Him the disciples of John, saying, why do we and the Pharisees fast oft, but thy disciples fast not?" The disciples of John came to Jesus and spoke to Him in such a way because they saw something—they saw Jesus sitting at a feast, not just an ordinary meal, but a feast (Luke 5:29). Furthermore, they saw Him feasting not with the high priests, the Pharisees, or the scribes, but with the sinners, the publicans. Jesus was feasting with the publicans, of all people. This really bothered the religious ones. Both John's disciples and the Pharisees came to Jesus, and the new-timers in religion took the lead to rebuke Him. "Why do we fast," they said, "but your disciples do not?" Why? Religiously speaking, the disciples of John and the disciples of the Pharisees were one hundred percent right: it is much better to fast than to feast. "Why do we fast and Your disciples feast?" they asked.

JESUS PRESENTS HIMSELF
AS THE BRIDEGROOM

The Lord Jesus did not argue nor reply to John's disciples and the Pharisees in a doctrinal way. He said to them, "Can the children of the bridechamber mourn, as long as the bridegroom is with them?" He answered not with a doctrine, but with a person. He referred to Himself as the Bridegroom! His presence causes them to rejoice, the presence of the Bridegroom. The Lord Jesus said nothing according to the teachings, according to the Scriptures, according to any quotation from the Bible in the old way. Neither did He say anything concerning Himself as the Almighty God, the Creator, the Lord or the Master. God in the religious concept is such a One, but the Lord Jesus mentioned nothing of this. On the contrary, He referred to Himself as a Bridegroom.

A Bridegroom is the most pleasant person in the entire universe. You say that you fear God, you want to please God, you like to serve the Lord, etc.—that is good, but it is rather religious. Have you ever had the concept that your Lord Jesus Christ is not only the most Holy God, the Creator, the Almighty Lord, and the Master, but He is your Bridegroom, the most pleasant person? In the presence of the Bridegroom, fear is nonexistent. He is so lovely; He is so pleasant; we need not fear such a One. Hallelujah, we have the Bridegroom! The Lord Jesus said that the Bridegroom is here, the most pleasant person is here. Suppose that when He replied to the disciples of John and the Pharisees in such a way John, James, and Peter suddenly shouted, Hallelujah! Do you think the Lord Jesus would rebuke them? Surely not; the Lord Jesus would be so happy.

The Lord Jesus is so much to us: He is the very God, He is the Creator, He is the Lord, He is the Master, He is the Lamb who bears away our sins and accomplishes redemption in a full way, and He is also the One with the Dove who imparts life into us and baptizes us with the Spirit. But, beside all these, He is the Bridegroom. Eventually, at the end of the Bible we have such a term, "the wife of the Lamb" (Rev. 21:9). This is a matter which is to some extent contrary to religion and religious thoughts. The Lamb is the Redeemer, but the Lamb who took away our sins on the cross is also our Bridegroom.

Some of you have been recently saved, while others have been saved for a considerable time. Have you ever prayed in this way, "O Lord Jesus, You are so lovely; You are my Bridegroom. Lord, I love You, I love You just as one who loves her bridegroom." Have you ever spoken to the Lord like this in your prayers? More or less we are under the influence of a religious concept. It is exceedingly easy for any Christian to pray, "O Lord. You are my God, You are my Father, You are my Master, You are my Creator." We could say this, but I fear we are not accustomed to saying, "Lord Jesus, You are my Bridegroom!"

THE BRIDEGROOM VERSUS
RELIGIOUS CONCEPT

Now we see the religious concept. Do not blame those Jewish people; we must blame ourselves. We have all become religious. We are still to some extent under religion's influence. We are talking about fasting and praying, while the Lord Jesus is saying, "Can the children of the bridechamber mourn as long as the bridegroom is with them?" The Lord Jesus is not speaking in doctrines or religious rituals, but pointing to Himself as the Bridegroom. Our God, our Creator, our Redeemer, our Lord and Master today is a Bride groom to us. We must all drop the religious concept and take up something new. I cannot force you, but I would ask you from this day to contact the Lord again and again with the sense that He is your Bridegroom. Would you? There is not much need to pray in the old religious way. I am afraid that when you forget God, you just forget Him; then, whenever you turn back to Him, you immediately pray in that old way. It is so easy to pray like that. But when you pray in the way of appreciating the Lord, it is entirely different. Do not think this is my teaching; it is the Lord's revelation. The Lord is going to recover it, and He is doing it now. We must have a change. Repent! Change your concept! Be buried! Enjoy Jesus as the Bridegroom!

Many times in my room by myself I have really become excited. The Lord is so much to me. He is so good, so wonderful, far beyond what I can express. He is the Bridegroom! Hallelujah! The Bridegroom is with us—we have His presence! We not only have the presence of the

Almighty God, but the presence of the Bridegroom, the most pleasant person. He is so precious and so lovely. The Lord Jesus must be like this to us.

In the matter of love, none of us keep any formalities or rituals. If we really love someone, we drop all the forms. If not, our love is not genuine. Therefore, since Jesus is our Bridegroom, we must drop all our rituals and formalities.

THE BRIDEGROOM'S PRESENCE

We need our concept radically changed. When we come to our meetings, the church meetings, we are coming to meet the Bridegroom. Whenever we come together, we are coming to be with our Bridegroom. His presence means everything to us. As long as He is with us, we need no regulations, no rituals, no doctrines or forms. Why does Christianity today need so many doctrines, forms, rituals, and regulations? Because they have lost the presence of the Lord. In a wedding we have the presence of the bridegroom, but in a funeral we have lost the presence of a dear one. In Christianity people have lost the presence of the dear One, so there is no excitement. But we have the presence of our Bridegroom, and His presence is everything to us. How could we help but be excited? We have to shout, we have to be exceedingly joyful. The Bridegroom is with us—Hallelujah!

CHILDREN OF THE BRIDECHAMBER

The Bible not only tells us that the Lord Jesus is our Bridegroom, but that as such a Person to us we are four kinds of people to Him. Matthew and Luke tell us that He is the Bridegroom, and we are the children of the bride chamber. We are the people who are with the Bridegroom in His chamber. We love the Bridegroom. In this sense, we are not the bride, but we are the children of the bridechamber. We gaze upon the Bridegroom; His presence is so good and pleasant to us. You see, the children of the bridechamber are certainly unlike those in the mortuary. We are not in a mortuary; we are in the bridechamber. Hallelujah! We are fellows of the Bridegroom in the bridechamber.

GUESTS AT THE WEDDING FEAST

Secondly, we are the guests invited by God to the wedding feast of His Son (Matt. 22:1-10; Rev. 19:9). God the Father is now preparing a wedding feast for His Son and inviting many to attend it. Hallelujah! We are not only the children of the bridechamber, but also the guests invited to the wedding feast. Have you not received an invitation? On the day you were saved you were invited by God the Father. "All things are ready," He said. "Come to the feast!" And we are feasting now. Praise the Lord, whenever we come into His presence, we realize that we have come to a feast. Whenever we come together in a meeting, we must realize that we have come to a wedding feast. The church meeting must not be just a meal, but a feast, and not an ordinary feast, but a wedding feast. Whose wedding? The Lamb's wedding. Do you come to the meetings for teaching or for learning? We must come to the meetings for feasting. Even while I am speaking in the meetings, I am feasting; I am feasting much more than you all. I do have a kind of enjoyment within my spirit. So in this sense, we are the guests invited to the wedding feast of the Lamb.

VIRGINS

Thirdly, we are the virgins going forth to meet the Bridegroom (Matt. 25:1-13). In one sense the Lord Jesus as the Bridegroom is with us, but in another sense He is away and is coming back. In one sense we are with Him and we are enjoying Him, but in another sense we are waiting for Him. And we wait for Him in the way of going forth to meet Him. We are the virgins. Whether I am male or female, as one going forth to meet the Bridegroom I am a virgin. We are all virgins going out of the world to meet Him. We are all virgins looking for His coming. That is our goal. He is the coming Bridegroom. We are the virgins—we love Him, we are waiting for Him, we are eagerly seeking His coming. We are the children of the bridechamber with the Bridegroom, we are the guests invited to His wedding feast, and we are the virgins going out of the world to meet Him.

We must realize that as virgins we are those who have nothing to do with this world. Our goal, our aim, is Christ; we are going forth to meet Him. If we are still involved in this earth, if our goal is something here, we all become gentlemen, not virgins. Sometimes I look at some of the sisters and say to myself, "You are a sister, but you are really a gentleman. You are full of earthly aims. Your aim is not the Bridegroom's coming. Your aim is something else, perhaps even your missionary work. You are pursuing some business other than the Lord Jesus." We all must be virgins and have nothing to do with this earth. Our goal is His coming, our goal is Christ; we are aiming at Him. As such, He is our real enjoyment. If you are not such virgins aiming at Christ, you miss at least a part of the enjoyment of Christ.

THE BRIDE

In the first sense we are the children of the bridechamber, in the second we are the guests, in the third we are the virgins, and in the fourth we are the bride. We are not only the children of the bridechamber, not only the guests invited to the wedding feast, not only the virgins waiting for Him, but eventually the bride herself! Hallelujah! (Rev. 19:7-8; 21:2, 9) Brothers and sisters, have you realized that He is so much to us, and we are so much to Him? Because He is so much to us, we must be so much to Him.

FOUR PERSONS TO ENJOY CHRIST
IN A FULL WAY

These four aspects are all for our enjoyment of Christ as our Bridegroom. In the first sense we are the fellows in the bridechamber enjoying the Bridegroom. In the second sense we are the guests enjoying Him as our feast. In the third sense we are the virgins enjoying the coming of the Bridegroom. And eventually, we will all be the bride to enjoy the Bridegroom to the uttermost. Thus, to enjoy Christ as the Bridegroom we must be four kinds of persons to Him. By all these four ways we enjoy Christ so richly and sweetly. May the Lord impress us deeply with all these four aspects and bring us into the full enjoyment of Christ.

If we would enjoy Christ in a full way, we must be one of the children of the bridechamber, one invited to the wedding feast, one of the ten virgins, and a part of the bride. We are waiting for the day when our Bridegroom will return and take us to be with Himself as His bride. That day has not yet come, but we may at least enjoy Him now in the first, second, and third ways. Sometimes, however, we do have a real foretaste of enjoying Him in the fourth way, as His very bride.

CHAPTER TWO

FOUR NEW THINGS

Scripture Reading: Matt. 9:14-17; Luke 5:33-39

We have seen how Christ presented Himself to the people as the Bridegroom. He said, "Can the children of the bridechamber mourn, as long as the bridegroom is with them?" In these words of His we see several things: firstly, that He is the Bridegroom, and secondly, that the Bridegroom is with us. You remember that in Matthew chapter 1 we are told that Christ was called Emmanuel, which means God with us. I really like these two words "with us." This does not mean that we have a certain doctrine or know the teaching, nor does it mean that we keep a kind of ritual or have any forms. It means that we have His very presence with us. His being with us means everything. Hallelujah, the Bridegroom is with us! Without His presence, everything is just religious. What does it mean to be religious? To be religious means to have all the scriptural things, all the fundamental things, and yet lack the presence of the Lord.

How wonderful it is to have the presence of the Bridegroom with us! Do you need comfort? Praise the Lord, His presence is your comfort. Do you need life? Praise the Lord, His presence is your life. Do you need anything else? I tell you, His presence is everything to you. If you have His presence, you have everything. Oh, the Bridegroom is with us!

The third implication of these words of the Lord is that He as the Bridegroom is with us that we may enjoy Him. How do we know this? Because He says, "Can the children of the bridechamber mourn?" The answer is obvious: we must be joyful; we cannot be otherwise in the presence of the Bridegroom Himself.

But the Lord did not stop here: He went on to amplify His statement by using some parables with much practical implication. First of all, He stated that no man puts a piece of new cloth upon an old garment. Following that, He tells us that neither do men put new wine into old wineskins. In the Gospel of Luke we have another item added: "No man putteth a piece of a new garment upon an old" (5:36). Thus, following the Lord's words regarding Himself as the Bridegroom, He presents us with four new things. They are full of significance. Firstly, we see the new cloth; secondly, the new garment; thirdly, the new wine; and lastly, the new wineskin. We have, therefore, the bridegroom with four new things.

The Lord's word is always so simple in clauses, phrases, and wording. But we must realize that the implication of the Lord's word is marvelous and profound. The words of the Lord are not like those of philosophers: they always use words very difficult to understand, and even after you understand them you have nothing. Praise the Lord, He is different. All His words are exceedingly simple—everyone is familiar with a new cloth, a new garment, new wine, and a new wineskin. But listen, the implication and significance of His words are profound. Eternity is required to comprehend them.

THE MEANING OF "NEW"

Here we have four things, and with each of them the single, unchanging word "new" is used. In the Greek, however, there are three different words used for this one English word. The word "new" as related to new cloth means "untreated" or "unfinished." One version for this passage translates the word "new" as "unshrunk." It is cloth which has never been dealt with, which has never been worked upon. This is the meaning of the word "new" in relation to the new cloth. The word "new" as related to the new garment and the new wineskin, however, means new in nature. In essence and in nature the garment and the wineskin are new. Lastly, the word "new" referring to the new wine means new in relation to time. This is wine which has just recently been made. In summary, the new cloth is cloth which is untreated and unfinished; the new garment and the new wineskin are materials which are essentially new in nature; and the new wine is something which has just been freshly brought forth. All these things are full of meaning.

THE NEW GARMENT

Why did the Lord Jesus, after telling us that He is the Bridegroom, go on to speak of these four new things—the new cloth, the new garment, the new wine and the new wineskin? We must look deeper to discern His meaning. The Lord tells us that the Bridegroom is with us. But look at yourself—do you deserve His presence? Do you think that your real condition in the eyes of God is worthy of the presence of the Bridegroom? We must all answer, "No." All we have and all we are does not deserve the Lord's presence. You see, to enjoy the Lord's presence we need certain qualifications; we need to be in a certain condition, in a certain situation. What we are by birth, what we are naturally, whatever we can do and whatever we have, does not qualify us to be in the presence of the Bridegroom. We must realize that the Bridegroom is Christ, and Christ is God Himself. Suppose that today God appeared to you. Could you just sit there? He is the Holy God, He is the righteous God; such a One is the Bridegroom. Do you remember the story in Luke 15? The prodigal son came home. The father undoubtedly loved him deeply, but the son's condition was utterly unbefitting to the presence of the father. Therefore, the father immediately told his servant to take the best robe and put it on him, thus to fit him for his presence. Our Bridegroom is God Himself. How may we, poor sinners, enjoy the presence of the heavenly King? You must remember the context of these verses in Matthew 9: the Lord Jesus was eating with sinners and publicans. We are the sinners and the publicans. We are not qualified; we need something to cover us that we may sit in the presence of the Lord. This is why, after the Lord spoke of Himself as the Bridegroom, He told us that we need to be clothed in a new garment. When we put on the new garment, we are worthy of His presence. When the prodigal son was clothed with the best robe, he could immediately stand in the presence of his honored father. The best robe qualified him to enjoy the father's presence. We as sinners and publicans do need to be clothed in a new garment that we may be worthy of the Bridegroom's presence. But this is not all.

THE NEW WINE

If I were the prodigal son, after putting on the best robe, I would be a bit concerned. I may say, "O father, the best robe satisfies you, but it does not satisfy me; I am still hungry. My outward situation now fits yours— that is fine for you. But what about me; I am hungry. I decided to come back to you, not for the best robe, but for some better food. When I was in that far land, I did not have even so much as the husks which the swine fed upon; so I decided to return to your house, not for this robe, but for something to eat. This robe satisfies you, father, but I need to be satisfied." Immediately the father told the servant to kill the fatted calf and said, "Let us eat and be merry." The father's provision is not just for something without, but also for something within.

Therefore, after the Lord spoke of the new garment, He immediately proceeded to speak also of new wine. The new wine is not a provision for the outward need, but for the inward need. We not only have an outward need, we also have an inward need. We need something to cover us, and we also need something to fill us. We are so poor outwardly, and we are so empty inwardly. We need the robe upon us for the Father's sake, but we need the new wine within us for our sakes. We need not only the new garment, but also the new wine.

We know that in a wedding feast, the most essential thing is the wine. Of course, when we go to the wedding, we dress in a new garment to fit the occasion. But we do not come just to sit down and look around. I do not come to look at your new garment and you at mine, yet without anything to eat or drink. Neither do we come to display our good etiquette. Of what use is it to practice table manners, yet have nothing to eat? Praise the Lord, we do have table manners, but we also need a rich table, and the Lord has provided it. The Lord is the new garment to us, and the Lord is also the new wine. Have you seen this? He is our covering, and He is also our content. He not only qualifies us, but He satisfies us as well. He is our qualification, and He is also our satisfaction; He is the provision for our outward need, and He is also the full provision for all our inward hunger and thirst.

If the Lord was not so much to us, how could we be the children of the bridechamber, the proper guests at the wedding feast, the virgins going forth to meet the Bridegroom, and the bride herself? In order to enjoy Christ in these four ways we need something outwardly to qualify us and something inwardly to satisfy us. Now the Lord Jesus is not only the Bridegroom, but also the new garment to qualify us and the new wine to satisfy us. We do have something to cover us, and we do have something to satisfy us. We can leap and shout, Hallelujah! But do not think this is all.

THE NEW WINESKIN

The new wine requires the new wineskin. What good is the new wine if there is no proper vessel to contain it, to preserve it? In ancient times the wineskin was used as a vessel to contain the wine. Therefore, the new wineskin signifies something that contains Christ as the new wine. What is this? This is the proper church life. Christ is not only our new garment and new wine, but, being increased, He is also our new wineskin to contain the wine. He is our outward qualification, He is our inward satisfaction, and He is in a corporate way the church, the Body (I Cor. 12:12), capable of holding the wine. He is everything. He is the Bridegroom, the new garment, the new wine, and also the corporate vessel to contain what we enjoy of Him. Christ enlarged is the new wineskin. The meaning here is indeed profound.

THE NEW CLOTH

We have spoken of three of the new items, but we have not indicated much concerning the new cloth. What is the significance of this? The Lord Jesus, we know, was God. One day He became incarnated as a man on this earth. From His incarnation to His crucifixion there were thirty-three and a half years in which He passed through all the human living. He was at that time the new cloth, untreated, undealt with either by man or by God. Christ incarnate, from His birth to His crucifixion, was the new cloth. Such a Christ is indeed wonderful, but not adequate, however, to cover us. Such a piece of cloth is indeed new, but not yet in a suitable condition for us to wear. It requires some cutting, some sewing, some work to be wrought upon it. All this was accomplished upon the cross. On the cross Christ was treated. He was crucified and He was buried: He was dealt with by man and even more so by God. After this, He was raised in resurrection. Now in resurrection He is the new garment. The resurrected Christ is the new garment. Before His crucifixion, He was a piece of new cloth, but after His resurrection He became a new garment for us to put on.

PUTTING ON THE NEW GARMENT
AND DRINKING THE NEW WINE

I do not like to present mere teachings and doctrines—I prefer the practice, the experience. Let me check with you: since after His resurrection Christ became the new garment, how then may we put Him on? How do you put

Him on? You should not forget Galatians 3:27, "As many
of you as were baptized into Christ did put on Christ."
We must put on Christ. Then by what way may we put
Him on? By being baptized into Christ. The way for us
to put on Christ is to be baptized into Christ. How may
we be baptized into Christ?

Up to this point, we are still dealing with doctrine. We
need something practical. We have seen that after His
resurrection Christ became a new garment, but the Bible
also tells us that after His resurrection He was made a
life-giving Spirit (I Cor. 15:45). If Christ were not the
Spirit, how could we be baptized into Him? Have you seen
the point? How can we be baptized into Christ? Because
Christ was made a Spirit. Christ, by being crucified,
buried and resurrected, was made a life-giving "pneuma,"
a life-giving breath, the living air. As the breath it is so
easy for Him to get into us, and as the air it is so easy
for us to get into Him. Christ in resurrection was made
a Spirit. This life-giving Spirit is the all-inclusive One. In
this Spirit is all that Christ is and all He has accomplished. This all-inclusive Spirit is the all-inclusive Christ
Himself, and this Christ as the Spirit is the new garment
for us to wear. You see, even this garment is the Spirit.
We were baptized into Christ as the Spirit—it is thus that
we put on Christ. Christ is the pneuma, the all-inclusive
Spirit; when we are baptized into Him, we put Him on.
Immediately He as the Spirit becomes our clothing, our
covering, and we are qualified. Hallelujah! So the new
garment which we must put on is Christ Himself as the
all-inclusive Spirit.

This is the meaning of the Lord's word in Matthew
28:19, "Go ye therefore, and disciple all nations, baptizing
them into the name of the Father, and of the Son, and
of the Holy Spirit." The reality of the name is in the
Spirit. To baptize people into the name means to baptize
them into the Spirit. And who is the Spirit? The Spirit is
just Christ as the all-inclusive pneuma. He became
incarnated, He lived on this earth, He was crucified and

accomplished redemption, and He was resurrected. After everything was finished, He became in His resurrection the all-inclusive pneuma. Incarnation is included in this pneuma; crucifixion and redemption are included in this pneuma; resurrection, the power of His resurrection, and the life of resurrection are all included in this pneuma. When we were baptized into Him, we were baptized into this pneuma. When we were baptized into Him, we put Him on. Hallelujah!

There is a marvelous verse in the New Testament, with words to which I am afraid you have paid little attention. It is I Corinthians 12:13. "For in one Spirit were we all baptized into one body, whether Jews or Gentiles, whether bond or free; and were all made to drink of one Spirit." It says firstly that we were all baptized in the Holy Spirit, and secondly that we were all made to drink of the one Spirit. We were not only baptized into the Spirit, but also made to drink of the Spirit. Have you noticed these two aspects in this one verse? Suppose I have here a glass of water. To baptize my finger in this water is one thing: the finger is clothed with the water; the water is put upon the finger. But this is just an outward act: something is put on, but not put in. The second aspect is that we are also made to drink the Spirit. When I drink this water in the glass, the water gets into me. To be baptized into is one thing, while to drink of is another.

Many Christians today confuse these two aspects, thinking that the baptism in the Spirit is equivalent to drinking of the Spirit. This concept is really not logical. When people are put into water, does that mean they are made to drink the water? If so, they will be drowned. To baptize a person is to put him into water, not to make him drink the water. There are two aspects. The Holy Spirit upon us is one thing, while the Holy Spirit within us is another. The Lord Jesus, when speaking to His disciples concerning the Holy Spirit on the Day of Pentecost (Acts 1:5, 8), said that the Holy Spirit would come upon them, not into them. It was a matter of "upon," not a matter of "in." To be baptized into the Spirit is to put on the Spirit, to put on Christ. Christ is our righteousness, Christ is our covering, Christ is our qualification, Christ is our new garment. But this should not be a mere doctrine. You must put on this Christ, not just receive the doctrine of justification by faith. It must be an experience in the Spirit. You should be able to exclaim, "O God, Hallelujah, I am now in Christ! Christ is the all-inclusive pneuma, and I am in the all-inclusive pneuma. I am standing before You, not in myself, but in Christ—not in Christ as a doctrine, but in Christ as the all-inclusive Spirit."

We must put on Christ as the new garment, and this new garment is the all-inclusive Spirit. Christ is no more the untreated cloth; He is now the finished garment. In this finished garment we have redemption, resurrection power, and all the divine elements of the divine Person. This new garment is not just a piece of clothing, but the divine pneuma, the all-inclusive Spirit, including Christ's incarnation, His crucifixion, His redemptive work, His resurrection, and His resurrection power. We can put on such a Christ. Hallelujah!

The Lord Jesus told His disciples, "I will pray the Father, and He shall give you another Comforter, that he may be with you forever; even the Spirit of reality" (John 14: 16-17). In these verses the Spirit is the treated Christ; this Spirit is the crucified and resurrected Christ. Such a Christ is the other Comforter, the Spirit of reality. "In that day," He said, "ye shall know that I am in my Father, and ye in me, and I in you" (John 14:20). He said in effect, "At that day you will both put Me on and receive Me into you. In that day you will be baptized into Me, and you will also drink of Me." This is the treated Christ, the finished Christ. Christ today is no more untreated; He has been thoroughly and completely worked upon. Now

He is the finished garment for us to put on, and now He is also the new wine for us to drink.

Suppose I have here an orange. Could you drink it? You could not—it is untreated, it must be dealt with first. We could not drink of Christ before His crucifixion and resurrection. On the cross He was cut and pressed by God, and now as the Spirit in resurrection we can drink of Him. We were all baptized into Christ, and we were also made to drink of Christ. How? Because He is now the treated Christ. He said, "If any man thirst, let him come unto me and drink. He that believeth on me, as the scripture hath said, from within him shall flow rivers of living water. But this spake he of the Spirit, which they that believed on him were to receive: for the Spirit was not yet" (John 7:37-39). Why at that time, when the Lord spoke those words, was the Spirit not yet? Because Christ was not treated yet. After a short time He would be treated, and then resurrected. Now, whoever thirsts may come unto Him and drink. Praise the Lord! Today the Lord Jesus is no more the untreated Christ. Do you want to be baptized into Him? Do you want to drink of Him? "That day" is this day. Today you may know that you are in Him and He is in you. You may be baptized in Him and you may drink of Him. Now, by being baptized into Him, Christ becomes our outward qualification, and now, by drinking of Him, He becomes our inward satisfaction. We are clothed with Him as the Spirit of power and we drink of Him as the Spirit of life that we may enjoy Him as our Bridegroom.

In the first three new things the new cloth, the new garment, and the new wine—we see Christ. Christ from His incarnation to His crucifixion is the new cloth, and Christ from His resurrection to eternity is our new garment and our new wine. The new cloth was just the material for making the new garment. Now we are daily under His covering. and we are daily satisfied by Him. He is everything to us.

CHRIST, THE NEW WINESKIN

Now we must see more concerning Christ as the new wineskin. Let us read I Corinthians 12:12, "For as the body is one, and hath many members, and all the members of the body, being many, are one body; so also is Christ." We read in this verse not only that the members composed together are the one Body, but that this Body is Christ. We always consider Christ as the Head; we have considered little, if at all, that Christ is also the Body. How, practically speaking, is Christ the Body? Because the Body is composed of so many members who are filled with Christ. Christ is in you, Christ is in me, Christ is in him, and Christ is in every one of us—we all have Christ within. Paul, in I Corinthians chapter 1, says that Christ is not divided. The Christ in you is one with the Christ in me, and the Christ in us is one with the Christ in all other Christians. So Christ is the Body composed of so many members who are filled with Him. This is the new wineskin. The new wineskin is simply the church life to contain Christ as the new wine.

Sometimes people condemn us by saying that we speak altogether too much about the church. But I do not think that we can ever talk too much about the church. I believe we will need eternity to exhaust it. Some say that whether we have the church or not, whether we are in the church or not, we can still enjoy Christ. But I do question whether you can fully enjoy Christ without the church. Without the church you may enjoy Christ here a little and there a little, but you can never enjoy Christ in a full way, neither can you enjoy Him constantly. If you do not agree, stay away from the church for a month and see what the result will be.

Many years ago a young brother came to me saying, "Brother Lee, I simply do not like the church life. Look at all those elders—I don't like them. Look at the leading sisters—I don't like them. Look at all those brothers and sisters—I don't like them." I replied, "All right brother, you don't like the elders, neither do you like the brothers and sisters. What about yourself?" He said, "Well, I'm not so good either, but I'm a little better than they are." He continued, "Why should I come to the church meetings—it's just a waste of my time. It would be much better for me to stay at home to pray and read the Bible." So I said, "All right brother, go and try it for a while and see what will result." Do you know what happened? For the first two weeks he did pray and read his Bible, but after that the Bible reading stopped, though he still prayed a little. After another week, the prayer ceased. Then he began attending the movies, and later went even deeper into the world.

Without the wineskin, how can you keep the wine? Do not consider that you yourself as an individual are the vessel. No, you are just a part of the vessel. How can a glass contain water if it is cut into pieces? How can the pieces contain the water? It is impossible. Do not consider that you are somebody. You are nobody. You are just a member of the Body; you are just a minute part of the Body. It is true, some amount of blood is in my little finger, but this little finger is just a part of the entire body. If you sever it from the body, the flow of blood in the finger immediately ceases. Instead of containing the blood, the finger will lose the blood. From the day you leave the church life, you begin to lose Christ, the new wine starts to run out. Check with your experience.

In so saying I do not infer that every meeting of the church life is so marvelous. Sometimes the church meetings are not so high. But even the experience of some low meetings is good for you. Whether a glass is held as high as the ceiling or as low as the floor, it is still a vessel. Whether it is up or down, it remains a container. The Lord Jesus always goes with this glass: when the glass goes higher, the Lord Jesus goes higher. When the church meetings go down, sorry to say, the Lord Jesus goes down with them. He must go with us, because He is in us. Nothing but the church life can contain the very Christ you enjoy. Do not think the church is a small thing.

Some who are reading this book are in places where there is as yet no church life. I believe that your experience, though it be on the negative side, will support my word. I fully sympathize with you. No doubt many of you are greatly concerned that there is no container, no wineskin, in your locality. You see, we need the new wine, and we also need the new wineskin.

We must also realize that the wineskin is not only the container of the wine, but also the means for us to drink the wine. Many of us can testify that whenever we came into the church meeting, we discovered that that was really the place where we could drink Christ. It was there that we began to drink the Lord as never before. The church life is not just a container, but a vessel from which we may drink. Praise the Lord, we have the church life.

The church life is not us; the church life is the corporate Christ. If I come here and leave my Christ at home, and if you come here just by yourself, that is not the church life, that is a kind of social club. Anything without Christ in it is not the church. However, if you come with Christ and I come with Christ, immediately this very Christ is the corporate container to contain Himself and dispense Himself for our enjoyment. The church life is not a religion or a set of teachings, forms and rituals, but Christ lived out from you and me.

A LIVING WINESKIN

Most all of us come from a background of Christianity, where we learned that Christians need to have certain kinds of Christian meetings called services. According to this concept everyone must enter the "sanctuary" quietly and reverently and seat himself properly and in order. Some dear ones who have attended our meetings have been exceedingly disturbed by the shouting and the praises. Let me say a word regarding them: they are unconsciously influenced by their background of Christianity. Suppose there are a number of Christians meeting together, everyone dressed nicely, everyone behaving quitly and properly. Suppose that in the same place there is another group of Christians not dressed so well, not behaving so orderly, but shouting and praising Christ. If you were Christ—be fair and honest—which group would you really appreciate? I do not mean which is right or wrong—I do not care for this, and I do not believe the Lord Jesus would care for this either. It is not a matter of being right or wrong, good or bad—it is a matter of life. Religion says the first group is good, but Christ says it is not good because it has no life. The first group is an insult to Christ. Christ is life, and Christ has conquered and subdued death. Christ would say to the first group, "Why is death so prevailing among you? Surely this is not like my church; this is like a cemetery." The most quiet and orderly place is the cemetery—there is no confusion there. Why? Because everyone is dead and properly buried. So many so called Christian churches today are just like that: everyone in them is nicely, properly and beautifully "buried." Brothers and sisters, that is not the new wineskin. The living church is where Christ is; it is the church composed of living members, making living noise. This is the new wineskin. We need such a wineskin.

NEW WINESKINS FOR NEW WINE

On one hand we have the old wineskin, and on the other hand we have the new. Do not put the new wine into the old wineskin. Some indeed have received the new wine, but they have attempted to bring the new wine back and pour it into the old wineskin. I have been witnessing this kind of folly for almost forty years. Many people have come to the local church and drunk the new wine. They have said, "This is really wonderful—this is just what 'my church' needs." So they have tried to bring this new wine back to that old wineskin. Do you know what happened? The old wineskins burst, and the new wine was spilled.

If we put the new wine into the new wineskin, however, the Lord Jesus said that both are preserved.

Some dear ones have come to appreciate the pray-reading; so they have tried to bring the pray-reading into their old meetings. They killed their meetings. The new wine simply does not fit in the old wineskins. The new wine requires the new wineskin.

We need Christ as the new garment, we need Christ as the new wine, and we also need Christ in a corporate way as the new wineskin. We need the church life. We do not care for any doctrine, teaching, or form, but just for Christ in you and Christ in me. This is the new wineskin.

FOUR KINDS OF CHRISTIANS

Out of these four new things, four kinds of so-called Christians have come into existence. The first kind are called Christians, but they are not really Christians. They only take Christ as the new cloth: they do not believe in the Lord's crucifixion or the Lord's redemption, but only appreciate the Lord while He was on this earth. They say, "Look how Jesus lived: He was so full of love and self-sacrifice. We must imitate Him, we must follow Him." But to do this is just to cut out a piece of new cloth with which to patch an old garment. These are the so-called modernists. They do not believe that Christ is God; neither do they believe that Christ died for our sins on the cross. They say that Christ died as a kind of martyr, not for our redemption, but to give us an example. We must imitate Him in certain aspects, they say, to patch up our holes. This is their teaching and practice.

Then there is another kind of Christians, a better kind, whom you may call fundamentalists. They believe that Christ is God, that Christ is our Redeemer, that Christ died on the cross for our sins and was resurrected. They take Christ not as a piece of new cloth, but as the new garment. They are redeemed, they are real Christians, but they only believe that Christ has accomplished redemption and that now they are saved and will go some day to heaven.

Then there is another group which is further improved. Some Christians have seen that they need not only the redemption of Christ, but also the life of Christ. They have realized something concerning the inner life; so they take Christ not only as the new garment, but also as the new wine. You may call them "inner life Christians." They are indeed an improvement over the previous two groups. You may say that they are the best—they are not modernists, and they are more than fundamentalists. You may even call them spiritual people. But I am sorry to say, good as they are, they lack one thing—the wineskin, the church life.

In the last days the Lord is recovering not only the new garment—this He recovered through Martin Luther in the matter of justification by faith. Neither is the Lord only recovering the inner life—this He accomplished through Madame Guyon, Andrew Murray, Jessie Penn-Lewis, etc. We thank the Lord for all these recoveries. However, at the end of this age the Lord is recovering the last and ultimate item, the church life. You may call this group the church people. Praise the Lord!

Have you ever noticed today that in the local churches, among the so-called church people, the new garment has been recovered, the new wine has been recovered, and the new wineskin has also been recovered. I do not believe the friends who criticize us for talking so much about the church are fair. We also speak very much concerning the new garment and even more about the inner life. Look into our writings—they are full of messages concerning the inner life. But we have not stopped there; we have also covered the church life. If you read all the books and papers we have published. you will discover that we are not occupied with the new cloth—that is over. But we do have the new garment, the new wine, and the new wineskin. We have Christ as our righteousness, we have Christ as our life, and we have Christ in a corporate way as our church life. Did the Lord stop with the new garment? No. Did the Lord stop with the new wine? No. The Lord went on from the Bridegroom to the new cloth, from the new cloth to the new garment, from the new garment to the new wine, and from the new wine to the new wineskin. Is there anything more? No. After the wineskin, after the church, there is nothing more. The church is God's ultimate goal. When we arrive at the church, we are in the ultimate consummation of God's purpose. Thus, after the wineskin, the Lord mentioned nothing else.

Praise the Lord! We have the Bridegroom, we have the new cloth made into the new garment, we have the new garment, we have the new wine, and we have the new wineskin. So we are not only fully qualified, not only fully satisfied, but also fully positioned to enjoy our Bridegroom. If we have experienced all these things, we are short of nothing. How wonderful to have the Bridegroom upon us as the new garment and within us as the new wine. And this new wine is in the church life, the new wineskin. Thus, day by day we have the full enjoyment of Him as the Bridegroom.

Is this religion? No. Is this Christianity? No. Is this a kind of new sect? No. Then what is this? It is the church life. Hallelujah! How wonderful to have it and be in it!

CHAPTER THREE

THE WAY TO REST

Scripture Reading: Matt. 11:18-19, 25-30; 12:1-14, 38-42

We have seen the matter of the Bridegroom with four new things in Matthew chapter 9. Now we come to chapters 11 and 12. The bridegroom is the most pleasant person that anyone could deal with. How pleasant it is to deal with our Bridegroom! That is our enjoyment. Chapter 9 tells us how to be pleasant, while here in chapters 11 and 12 we learn how to obtain genuine rest.

All the passages in Matthew chapters 11 and 12 are closely connected. Notice the words "At that time" in chapter 11, verse 25 (King James Version). Throughout the entire Bible, little words like these are very significant. God's Word is very economical—there are no wasted words. Let us consider the words in chapter 11, verse 25, "At that time." At what time? At the time Jesus said that John came neither eating nor drinking. The religious people said that John had a demon, and that the Son of man, because He came both eating and drinking, was a glutton and a winebibber (Matt. 11:18-19). Then "at that time" Christ sounded out His call: "Come unto me, all ye that labor and are heavy laden, and I will give you rest" (v. 28).

Following chapter 11, in the first verse of chapter 12, we again encounter the same three words, "At that time." At what time? At the time Jesus sounded His call, at the time Jesus invited people to come unto Him and rest.

Following this passage at the beginning of chapter 12, we come to verse 38, which opens with a little word,

"Then." All these little words join all the portions in these two chapters together. We may say, therefore, that these two chapters are one whole, showing us one thing—how to find rest.

Would you find full enjoyment? Would you be pleasant? Then be in the presence of the pleasant One; be in the presence of the Bridegroom. As long as we have our Lord Jesus, our Bridegroom, with us, we cannot but rejoice. Now from all these portions in chapters 11 and 12, we see something more—we see how to find rest.

Christians are accustomed to quoting Matthew 11:28, "Come unto me, all ye that labor and are heavy laden...," but they usually quote and use these verses in an isolated way. We need to put all the passages of these two chapters together in order to find the way to rest.

LIFE VS. REGULATIONS

John came neither eating nor drinking. He behaved utterly contrary to religion and human culture, and because of this the Pharisees and scribes, the religious people, said that he had a demon. John was indeed a strange person. They could not understand him; so they said he had a demon. Then Jesus came both eating and drinking, and the religious people said, "Look, this man seems to know nothing but eating and drinking."

If any regulation is made saying that we should not eat or drink, it becomes a heavy burden. On the other hand, if any rule is made saying that we must eat and drink large amounts of food and liquid, this also becomes a heavy burden. But to us, the children of wisdom, it is not a matter of abstaining from food and drink, neither is it a matter of eating and drinking, but absolutely a matter of life. Notice the Lord's words in verse 19 of this chapter: "Wisdom is justified of her children" (King James Version). We need to be impressed with the word "children." This is a matter of life. We are not students of wisdom, but children of wisdom. We do not care so much for the knowledge of wisdom, but we care very much for the life of wisdom. What is wisdom? Christ is wisdom. We are the children of Christ; we have the life of Christ; so we have the life of wisdom. To us it is not a matter of regulations—do this, and do that, etc. It is not a matter today of so many do's and don't's, but entirely a matter of life. If I am thirsty, I may drink: I may drink little by little, or I may drink a quantity of liquid at once. There is no regulation. It all depends on life. Do not ask me why I drink—my answer is only that I am thirsty. When I am thirsty, do not give me any regulation that I should not drink. And when I am not thirsty, do not command me to drink. Do not ask me why I eat so much—it is because I am hungry. Neither ask me why I do not eat—it is because I am not hungry. What is this? This is life. This is the way to find rest. Regulations and rules are a heavy burden, and Jesus said, "Come unto me, all ye that labor and are heavy laden, and I will give you rest."

Hallelujah, there are no regulations! Are you hungry? Then eat! Are you thirsty? Drink! If you are not hungry or thirsty, do not eat or drink. You see, as long as we do not have any regulations, we are free, we have rest.

All the regulations of religion are just the heavy burden of verse 28. This is why the Lord Jesus exclaimed, "Come unto me, all ye that labor and are heavy laden..." There is no need for you to labor. Forget about regulations: eating or not eating, drinking or not drinking—forget them all. When it is convenient, I will eat, and when it is not convenient, I will not eat. When I am thirsty I will drink, and when I am not thirsty, I will not drink. Hallelujah, there are no regulations! This is Christ versus religion. Jesus said, "My yoke is easy" (11:30). In the Greek the meaning of the word "easy" is "kindly" or "gentle." In other words Jesus said, "My yoke is flexible." When you are hungry you eat, and when you are not hungry you do not eat. His yoke is flexible, His yoke is gentle, His yoke is not unbending.

JESUS INTENTIONALLY BREAKS THE SABBATH

It was "at that time," after speaking in this way, that Jesus went with His disciples on the sabbath day through the cornfields. The disciples saw all the ears of corn, and because they were hungry they all began to help themselves and eat. The Pharisees, however, saw it and said, "Behold, thy disciples do that which it is not lawful to do upon the sabbath" (12: 2). You see, to keep the sabbath day in such a way is really a heavy burden. Jesus said, "Come unto me, all ye that labor and are heavy burdened." Any regulation, any rule, is a kind of burden. But with Christ there are no regulations, no rules. Consider the situation: the Lord Jesus took the hungry ones out of the synagogue, perhaps; out of something religious, and into the cornfield. Do you think He did this without meaning? I tell you, the Lord Jesus did this intentionally with a purpose. He deliberately broke the observation of the sabbath day in order to satisfy those who were hungry. Religion burdened them; the Lord Jesus satisfied them.

Religious people are always like this. They are always putting burdens upon others and not allowing others to eat. They are always saying it is not lawful, it is not fundamental, it is not according to the Scriptures. But the Lord Jesus said, "Have you not read?" He said in effect, "You are so fundamental, you are so scriptural, have you not read what David did when he was hungry, and they that were with him; how he entered into the house of God and ate the shewbread, which it was not lawful for him to eat, neither for them that were with him, but only for the priests? Have you not read that, you Pharisees? According to your law, it was not lawful for David or his followers to eat, but they ate." Those scriptural people, those fundamental people, were shut up. It is very meaningful.

CHRIST, THE REAL DAVID

Christ is everything versus religion. There was indeed such a regulation in the law, saying that only the priests

were allowed to eat the shewbread in the house of God.
Yet in the same Bible which records this regulation is a
record telling how David entered the temple and together
with his followers ate the shewbread. And God did not
condemn them. The Lord Jesus in so speaking was telling
the Pharisees, "I am the real David, and my disciples are
the real followers of the real David. If in the ancient time
David and his followers ate the shewbread, which they
were not allowed to eat, and were not condemned, how
can you condemn Me? You must realize that David was
only a type, a shadow, a figure—I am the real David. If
whatever David did was lawful, then whatever I do must
be lawful. If you go into the temple by yourself, without
David, and eat the shewbread, you will be condemned. It
is by David being with you, it is by being in the presence
of David, that whatever you do is lawful. It is not a matter
of the law, but a matter of David."

Now in this present day, it is not a matter of the law,
but wholly a matter of Christ. As long as Christ is with
you, as long as you do something in the presence of Christ,
it is all right. Why? Because Christ today is the present,
instant, and up-to-date lawgiver. Hallelujah! Christ is
today's real David, and we are His followers. We have Him
with us, and we are doing things in His presence.

There are no regulations today, but Christ. There are
no regulations, but the real David. As long as I am
following my David today, as long as I am one with my
Christ, whatever I do in His presence is all right. Could
you say this? Do you have the vision to say this?

CHRIST,
THE GREATER TEMPLE

Then the Lord Jesus said something more. He said,
"Have ye not read...?" (12:5). Do not think you understand
the Bible more than the Lord Jesus. Again the Lord Jesus
checked with them, "Have ye not read in the law, that on
the sabbath day the priests in the temple profaned the
sabbath and are guiltless?" It is even legal for the priests

to break the sabbath. As long as they are in the temple
there is no bondage, they are free from the law. If they
are outside the temple, they must keep the sabbath, but
if they are in the temple, they are liberated. The temple
is their emancipation. The Lord Jesus said, "I say unto
you, that one greater than the temple is here" (v. 6). The
Lord Jesus was saying in effect to the Pharisees, "My
disciples were eating in the Temple. They were breaking
the sabbath in Me, in today's greater Temple. As long as
they are in Me, whatever they do is right. What have you
got to say? Do you really think you know the Bible? I tell
you, Pharisees and scribes, you know just a little. You
really do not know the Bible so well. Have you not read?
The priests were allowed to profane the sabbath in the
temple. Now I am the greater Temple, and all my disciples
are the priests in Me. Whatever they do, even if it is
against the law, it is not actually against the law because
they are in the Temple. So they are free."

If you are outside the Temple, you are bound, but if
you are in the Temple, you are free. If you are outside
Christ, you are under bondage, but if you are in Christ,
you are free. It is marvelous! Christ is not only the Temple
today, but the greater Temple. Isn't this good? You can
never beat the Lord Jesus. Do not come to Him to try to
win your case. Strictly speaking, you do not have a case.
Don't say you have lost your case—you never had a case
to begin with. Jesus has all the cases. "Have you not read
about David?" "Have you not read about the priests in the
temple?" "Have you not read?" So shut up.

CHRIST,
THE LORD OF THE SABBATH

The Pharisees said that it was not lawful to eat the
corn because it was the sabbath. Eventually the Lord
Jesus told them, "The Son of man is Lord of the sabbath"
(v. 8). The Lord Jesus said in effect, "I had the right in
the ancient time to establish the sabbath, and today I
have the right to do away with the sabbath. What is wrong

with that?" On my left wrist I have a watch. It is my watch. In the morning I put it on. Now suppose I feel like taking it off. What can you say? It is my watch; I do what I want with it. I am the lord of the watch. If I want to put it on, I put it on; if I want to take it off, I take it off. Even so, the Lord Jesus said, "I am the Lord of the sabbath." He said by implication, "I am Lord not only of the sabbath, but of you too." Hallelujah!

If I have Christ, I have the real David. If I have Christ, I have the greater Temple. Hallelujah! If I have Christ, I have the Lord of the sabbath. It is really good. His name is "I am." What can we say, but, "O Lord, Amen, Hallelujah!"

CHRIST HEALS
THE WITHERED MEMBER

Have you seen that Christ is versus religion? But listen, this is just the first sabbath. Following this, there is another sabbath in chapter 12. After the first sabbath was over, the Lord Jesus went into the synagogue on the sabbath day, where there was a man with a withered hand. The religious people then took the opportunity to trouble the Lord Jesus again by asking, "Is it lawful to heal on the sabbath day?" (v. 10). Here was a case of a man with a withered hand—not a case of a whole man, but a case of a member of the body, a hand. It is quite meaningful. In the first sabbath the Lord Jesus took care of Himself as the Head of the Body. Now in the second sabbath the Lord needs to take care of His members. Here is a withered hand, a withered member nearly dead. The Lord answered the Pharisees, "What man shall there be of you, that shall have one sheep, and if this fall into a pit on the sabbath day, will he not lay hold on it, and lift it out? How much then is a man of more value than a sheep!" (12:11-12). He said in other words, "What is wrong then if I heal this withered member?" The hand is a member of the body, and the sheep is a member of the flock. Have you seen this? On this sabbath the Lord indicated that He would do anything for the healing of His members, for the rescue of His fallen sheep. Sabbath or no sabbath, the Lord is interested in healing the dead members of His Body. Regulations do not matter to the Lord; but the rescue of His fallen sheep means very much to the Lord. The lesson from the first sabbath is that the Head is everything, Christ is everything—Christ is David, the greater Temple, and the Lord of the sabbath. But in the second sabbath the lesson is that the Lord Jesus does not care for anything but His withered members, His fallen sheep. It is very meaningful.

Christianity today cares for regulations—they do not care for Christ, the Head. Christians today care for their formalities, doctrines, and rules—they do not care for the withered members of the Body of Christ, they do not care for the sheep of the flock.

In the beginning of 1968 something really happened in Los Angeles. The burial. It was the time of the New Year Conference, and I had no intention of encouraging people to be buried. But at the closing of one meeting, one said, "I want to be buried." Then others followed until many brothers and sisters in the church were buried. They were all so deeply moved to testify by this act that they were burying all their oldness, and by doing this they became alive. I was really surprised by this move to be buried. I was trying, in fact, to say some word to stop it, but I was checked by the Spirit within. Who was I to stop something of the Holy Spirit? I said not a word until the third day, when I predicted that the church in Los Angeles would certainly be criticized by the religious people for this act. It was not more than ten days before the criticism came. "There is heresy in Los Angeles," they said. "Believers who are already properly baptized are being baptized again. Where is the scriptural ground for a believer to be baptized again after being properly baptized already?" I do not like to argue, but I wish to tell you that so many withered "hands" were healed. Not only did this occur in Los Angeles, but following this in many

places, many dead ones through this kind of burial came
alive. What can we say?

Poor Christianity! They do not care if you are withered
or alive as long as you keep the regulations. If you keep
the "sabbath" with a withered hand, they do not care. But
where is the rest? There is no rest for a withered member.
The Lord Jesus said in effect, "I do not care for the
sabbath; I just care for My members, My fallen sheep."
The religious people say, "Look, we are so sound, we are
so scriptural, we have everything in order." But the Lord
Jesus would say, "I'll have none of it. I only care to heal
my members and rescue my sheep." The Lord Jesus did
not care for all the regulations. What does it mean to
keep the sabbath? Nothing. But to heal a withered hand
really means something. To lift the fallen sheep out of
the pit really means something. If so many hundreds of
people were made alive by being buried, what can you
say?

Some say our meetings are too noisy. They cannot bear
our shouting and praising. But look at the fruit. Today,
if you go to the so-called Christian churches in America
on Sunday morning, it is rather difficult to find many
under the age of thirty. They are mostly all old people.
But most of us here are under the age of thirty. We have
so many young people who have sold themselves for the
Lord's recovery. They care for nothing but Christ as the
Head and the Church with all the members as the Body.
If so, what would you say? Oh, bury the old dead religion!
You have been in it for years as a withered member.

The Lord does not care if people are noisy. A number
of times in the Psalms, it says, Make a joyful noise unto
God (66:1; 81:1; 95:1, 2; 98:4, 6; 100:1). God is a God of
the living, not of the dead. Living ones must be noisy;
only the dead ones are quiet. There is no need to command
the dead to be quiet; they are quiet because they are dead.
Today is not the age of formalities; today is not the age
of religion. Today is the age of the living Christ and the
living members; not the Christ in teachings and doctrines,

but the Christ in life, the Christ as the life-giving Spirit. Look at all these young people who are sold out for Christ and the Church. They will burn the whole country for the Lord.

The Lord cares for Himself as the Head, and He also cares for all His members. He will cure the withered members, He will rescue the fallen sheep. He will make a living church, not a formal church. Hallelujah, the hungry disciples were fed, and the man with the withered hand found rest, the sheep fallen into the pit was rescued. "Come unto me, all ye that labor and are heavy laden, and I will give you rest." This means negatively that He will take away all the regulations, and positively that He will give us food, healing, rescue, and rest. He is the only way for us to find rest. Rest is not in anything religious; religion burdens us. Christ is our rest. His yoke is gentle, and His burden is light. Why? Because it is a matter of life. Anything of life is so gentle and easy to bear.

CHRIST,
THE GREATER JONAH

Now in chapter 12 again another religious matter is presented to the Lord Jesus. "Then certain of the scribes and Pharisees answered him, saying, Teacher, we would see a sign from thee" (v. 38). A sign is a miracle; it is something accomplished miraculously. The Lord Jesus, of course, performed a good number of miracles while He was on this earth. But when the religious people came and asked Him to perform some miracle, He would not do it. This means that the Lord Jesus never performs any miracle in a religious way. Humanly speaking, all people like to see miracles. To have this kind of disposition or inclination is entirely natural and religious. If today the Lord would perform a miracle in our midst, we would all be excited—that is wholly a natural and religious reaction. When the scribes and Pharisees asked the Lord for a miracle He answered, "An evil and adulterous generation seeketh after a sign; and there shall no sign be given to it but the sign of Jonah the prophet: for as Jonah was three days and three nights in the belly of the whale; so shall the Son of man be three days and three nights in the heart of the earth" (vv. 39-40). The Lord said that He would not do any miracle for them; He just referred them to the sign of the prophet Jonah. Jonah spent three days and three nights in a whale, and eventually came out—that was undoubtedly a kind of miracle, but it was not a miracle accomplished in a religious way. Jonah's miracle was a miracle wrought in the way of resurrection—a picture of the resurrected Christ. Christ was put into the heart of the earth, even deeper than the belly of the big fish. After three days and three nights He emerged in resurrection. This resurrection is Christ; this Christ in resurrection is the unique miracle for today.

The natural and religious thought of man is that if we could perform miracles we could certainly build a good church. Never. Through the miracles which the Lord performed while He walked on earth multitudes were attracted to Him. But eventually, following the Lord's ascension, there were only one hundred and twenty together in the upper room (Acts 1:15). I believe that represented less than one out of a thousand of those who flocked around the Lord in the Judean and Galilean villages and countryside. At just one miracle of His, five thousand besides the women and children were fed (Matt. 14:21). Even after the Lord's resurrection, He appeared at one time to five hundred brothers (I Cor. 15:6). Yet, after His ascension, only one hundred and twenty were gathered together. Where were the others? Only those who really had some experience of the resurrected Christ as their life were the steadfast ones. The only thing that can build us into the church is not a miracle, but resurrected life, the resurrected Christ.

Here we have a case of people coming to the Lord and asking for a sign. But the Lord Jesus answers that there will be no sign, no miracle. The unique sign is that of resurrection, the resurrected Christ. We all must know, experience, possess, and be possessed by the resurrected Christ. Even Paul, near the end of his journey, expressed his longing desire to know Christ and the power of His resurrection (Phil. 3:10), not the miracles. He himself had performed quite a number of miracles during his lifetime, but he did not count on that. He only wanted to know Christ and His resurrection power. It is not an outward miraculous matter, but an inward resurrection matter. It is not a matter of signs, wonders, and miracles, but a matter of the powerful, resurrected Christ. We need to see the resurrected Christ.

CHRIST,
THE GREATER SOLOMON

Following the Lord's reference to Jonah, He spoke of Solomon. According to historical sequence, Solomon preceded Jonah. But here, according to spiritual sequence, Jonah precedes Solomon. What Jonah typifies of the Lord Jesus comes first; what Solomon typifies of the Lord Jesus follows. Jonah typifies Christ as the resurrected One; Solomon typifies Christ as the One in resurrection with wisdom to accomplish God's eternal purpose, to build up God's house, the temple, and to rule over God's kingdom. Our Christ is firstly today's Jonah, and secondly today's Solomon. He is the resurrected One, and He is the One in resurrection with wisdom to build God's house and rule over God's kingdom, thus accomplishing God's economy. What we need is not signs or miraculous things, but the resurrected Christ as our resurrection life to build up God's house, to fulfill God's purpose, and accomplish God's economy.

THE LORD'S PRESENT RECOVERY

I am really happy with the Lord's grace shown in the church in Los Angeles. Some dear ones have come to our meetings and after staying for some time have made the following comment: "It is really strange—you people do not speak in tongues, yet your meetings are more living than the meetings of those who speak in tongues." They never believed that people who do not speak in tongues could have such living meetings. The dear one who made this observation in Los Angeles also made the same observation in the church in Houston. "Even we who speak in tongues," he said, "do not have such meetings." The Lord Jesus never cares for any forms, ways, or traditions— the Lord Jesus only cares for Himself.

Now the age of the doctrines and gifts is over. We do not mean that today we do not have the doctrines or the gifts. We all know that the Lord's recovery began with Martin Luther. The unique item of the Lord's recovery at that time was the matter of justification by faith. We can say now—and I believe we are all clear concerning this—that the age of the recovery of justification by faith is over. This does not mean that we do not need justification by faith. Following Martin Luther, the matter of sanctification by faith was also recovered. If you read the history of the Lord's recovery, you will realize that at a certain period many of the Lord's servants, including John Wesley, paid their full attention to the matter of holiness. The matter of sanctification or holiness was fully recovered. A little later, the matter of the inner life was also recovered. These are all various stages or ages of the Lord's recovery. The first stage of His recovery was that of justification by faith. This was followed by item after item, age after age. It was at the end of the last century and the beginning of this century that the Pentecostal experience was also recovered. It is difficult to trace its origin: some say it began with the Welsh revival in 1903 and 1904; others say it began earlier than this. In any case, the Lord accomplished a definite recovery through the so-called Pentecostal movement. To some, the term "Pentecostal" does not have a good connotation. But it is a scriptural term, a good term; it is something of the Lord's recovery. In that recovery there were undoubtedly many genuine miraculous manifestations. But we all must

realize that just as the stage of justification by faith is
over, so also is the age of the recovery of the Pentecostal
movement over. This does not mean, however, that we do
not need the Pentecostal experience or the things related
to it. What we mean is that the Lord is going on to
accomplish a further recovery, a recovery of Christ, the
Spirit, and the church life. This is the age of such a
recovery.

We are not saying that we do not need all the previous
items. Hallelujah, we have inherited all the foregoing
matters! In the church life we have justification by faith,
in the church life we have sanctification by faith, in the
church life we also have the other items of the Lord's
recovery, including the Pentecostal experience. What I
mean is this: if we put our stress on any one of these
things, we are wrong. If today we are only stressing and
emphasizing the matter of justification by faith, we are
four or five hundred years behind the time. If we are so
preoccupied with the age of the Pentecostal movement,
we are at least three quarters of a century out of date.
Please do not misunderstand and think that we are
opposing justification by faith or any other items of the
Lord's past recovery. We are not against the genuine
speaking in tongues or the Pentecostal gifts. No, not at all.
We are just for the church, the all-inclusive church, not the
denominations, not the sects founded on particular items.
The Lutheran Church was founded on the doctrine of
justification by faith. The Holiness churches were founded
on the doctrine of holiness. The so-called Pentecostal
churches were founded on the Pentecostal experience. But
the church is founded on none of these things. The church
is founded on the all-inclusive, unique unity of all
believers.

The age of the Lord's recovery today is the age of
Christ as life, as the life-giving Spirit, and the church
life. By experience we can say that there is no other way
the local churches could be built up solidly and livingly
but by Christ as life in our spirit. What we should be

experiencing now day by day is the greater Jonah and the greater Solomon: the greater Jonah to be our resurrection life, and the greater Solomon to accomplish God's eternal purpose by building up His house and then His kingdom. Hallelujah, today we have Christ as the greater Jonah and the greater Solomon!

In this wonderful portion of Matthew, we have Christ as 1) today's David, 2) the greater Temple, 3) the Lord of the sabbath, 4) the greater Jonah, and 5) the greater Solomon. If you have Christ as all these items, you will have rest. The Lord Jesus said, "Come unto Me, all ye that labor and are heavy laden, and I will give you rest. My yoke is gentle, and my burden is light." He said, in other words, "Just come to Me; I am your David who can afford you full satisfaction, I am the greater Temple in which you may be free from all kinds of bondage and regulations, I am the Lord of the sabbath who can give you rest and who is your rest, I am the greater Jonah that affords you something of the resurrection, and I am the greater Solomon, continually accomplishing God's economy in you, through you, and among you." Where else could we find rest? This is the only way.

I know of some evangelists, missionaries, and Christian workers who work strenuously day by day in their evangelistic work. Yet while they are working, they do not have rest. I am not criticizing, I am stating the fact. If they would honestly reveal their experience, they would admit that they are not at rest. Then you may turn the question to me: "What about you, brother?" I can tell you by the Lord's grace that I work very much, but all the day I am resting. I am so happy, so very happy. I have the greater Jonah with the greater Solomon. I have Christ as my resurrection life and I am in the accomplishment of God's eternal economy. Hallelujah, there is nothing better than this!

CHAPTER FOUR

REVELATION, VISION, AND APPLICATION

Scripture Reading: Matt. 16:13-19, 17:1-9, 24-27

For a considerable number of years we have been abiding mostly in the Epistles—in Ephesians, Romans, and all the other letters written mostly by the Apostle Paul. Sometimes we have been in the Gospel of John. How we have loved all these books! But this year the Lord has opened the book of Matthew to us and we have received something new. I myself love the book of Matthew and cannot keep away from it. Oh, I do have a burden to recommend Matthew to you! We all must love Matthew.

We have seen how Matthew gives a record of Jesus as the Bridegroom with all the other items—the new cloth, which was good for making the new garment, the new wine, and the new wineskin. We cannot find all these precious items in the other books of the New Testament. I know you love the Gospel of John, but you cannot find the new garment, the new wine, or the new wineskin in John. Formerly, I loved John very much, perhaps more than you, but today I find something more in Matthew. John is rich, but John is not all-inclusive. I tell you, Matthew is all-inclusive. Matthew is so precious.

THREE STEPS OF ONE EXPERIENCE

Now we come to chapter 16 and 17 of Matthew, and from these two chapters we will gather three portions: chapter 16:13-19, chapter 17:1-9, and chapter 17:24-27. If you pray-read these three portions carefully, you will see that they give you three steps of one experience. With all spiritual things, if we would experience them, we need these three steps. What are they?

In the first portion, chapter 16:13-19, the Lord used the word "revealed." "Flesh and blood hath not revealed it unto thee, but my Father who is in heaven" (v. 17). This means that the first step to experience anything of the Lord is revelation. Revelation is more than knowledge, more than understanding; it is the realization of something deeply within. In this first portion of these two chapters Peter and the other disciples obtained a revelation. Then, in the second portion, in chapter 17:1-9, the Lord Jesus mentioned the word "vision." "Jesus commanded them, saying, tell the vision to no man, until the Son of man be risen from the dead" (v. 9). The second step, therefore, of experiencing something of Christ is further and deeper than revelation—it is vision. What is the difference between revelation and vision? The word "revelation" in the Greek means an unveiling. When a veil is taken away from any object, you can see it—this is revelation. Nevertheless, I may take away the veil, but there may be no light. Furthermore, I may take away the veil, but you may be born blind. So we need the revelation, the unveiling, and we also need the light plus the sight. Then we have the vision. We not only need a revelation, but also a vision.

My job in all these messages is to take away the veils. One by one I am taking them away. In the last message I took away a veil; in this message I will take away another veil. I want you to see this wonderful Person; so I am taking away veil after veil. You may think that as long as the veils are removed, surely you will be able to see. But, I tell you, I can only take away the veils, I cannot shine upon you. Light comes from the heavens; light comes from the very God who commands the light to shine in darkness. I cannot do that; I am not God. Receive the mercy of God, however, and the light will immediately shine upon you. Yet you still need something more—you need sight. You need not only the light, but also the sight.

These three added together give you the vision—the unveiling, the light, and the sight.

The first step to experience Christ is to obtain revelation. Then following this, we need vision. Yet, even after we have taken the second step, we do not have the real experience. Therefore, we must look into the third portion of these two chapters, in chapter 17:24-27, where we see the application. The third step is the application. After the revelation, we need the vision, and following the vision, we need the application. We must realize something. and even more we must see that very thing, but how to apply it is yet another matter. I cannot help you with this. All I can do, I say again, is take away the veils; God, then, by His mercy can shine from the heavens and give you sight to receive the vision; then after the vision. you need to apply it. You need to know how to apply what you have seen. Peter firstly obtained the revelation and secondly the vision, but thirdly he learned the application in such a hard way that it could never be forgotten. The harder it is to learn, you know, the harder it is to forget. Peter could never forget this lesson. Hallelujah, the Lord got through and Peter got through also! I do not mean that Peter was able to get through, but that the Lord was able to bring him through. The Lord brought him through the revelation, through the vision, and through the application.

Let us look into all these three steps. What was the revelation? What was the vision? And what was the application Peter learned?

THE REVELATION

Outside of religion

Matthew always gives a hard time to the religious people. Everything that Matthew tells us concerning Christ is outside of religion. In the first portion of Matthew 16 we read, "Jesus came into the parts of Caesarea Philippi..." (v. 13). If you look at the map, you will see that Caesarea Philippi was far to the north, even

north of Galilee. It was at the farthest extreme of the
region of Palestine. Isaiah 9:1 tells us that the land of
Galilee was of the Gentiles. But this place was even
further than Galilee; so it was more gentile. It was almost
outside the Holy Land; at best we could say that it was
on the border. In those days there was the holy place, the
holy temple, the holy city, and the holy land—a four-fold
holy sphere. Jesus kept Himself away from every one of
them. The holy things in those days were the religious
things. By the term "four-fold holy" is meant four times
religious. The land was religious, the city was religious,
the temple and all the things within it were religious.
Jesus came into the parts of Caesarea Philippi and got
away from all of them.

Jesus did not bring His disciples into the city of
Caesarea Philippi; He was there just in the parts, the
area, the district of that place. In that totally gentile
setting He asked His disciples, "Who do men say that the
Son of man is?" In other words, "Who do those people in
the religious circle say that I am?"

If we would see or learn something of the Lord Jesus,
we must be removed from religion. If you still remain in
religion, in any of the denominations or so-called Christian churches, it is difficult for you to receive any
revelation. You must leave all the religious things. In the
temple the priests were praying, offering their sacrifice,
burning the incense, lighting the lamp, etc.—whatever
they did was altogether religious; whatever could be seen
was nothing but religion. The Lord Jesus took His disciples
out of the priesthood, out of the temple, out of the city,
and out of the Holy Land. He asked, "Who do men say
that the Son of man is?" And they answered, "Some say
John the Baptist; some, Elijah; and others, Jeremiah, or
one of the prophets" (16:14). They answered with the
names of all the religious "big shots." This is the way the
religious people spoke of Jesus. Their realization concerning the Lord Jesus was wholly religious. The Lord never
appreciates this kind of realization.

Revelation of Christ

Then the Lord Jesus turned to His disciples and told them in effect to forget all that religious realization. He asked, "Who say ye that I am?" And Simon Peter answered, "Thou art the Christ, the Son of the living God" (v. 16). According to the record of the four Gospels, Peter was nearly always mistaken. There was only one time he was right—this was the time. Peter was one who always took the lead. A person who is so quick to take the lead will surely make many mistakes. Peter was this kind of person, always putting his foot in his mouth. This time, however, he was one hundred percent right. He called Jesus "the Christ, the Son of the living God." This is revelation.

Revelation of the church

Peter had seen the revelation of Christ, and the Lord Jesus appraised him well. But in the following verse, the Lord Jesus said, "And I also say unto thee..." (v. 18). Peter had just received the first fifty percent of the revelation. The revelation He had seen was utterly right, but it came short. Peter had seen who Christ was—that was wonderful, but it was not sufficient. You must underline the little word "also" in the beginning of verse 18—it is tremendously significant. In using this word the Lord Jesus, in effect, was saying unto Peter, "What you have seen is absolutely correct, but it is just fifty percent, just the first half; you still need the second half." Then Jesus proceeded to speak to Peter about the church. The first half of God's divine revelation is Christ, and the second half is the church. The first half is the Head, and the second half is the Body.

If you would see a person, and his head only is unveiled, your revelation is not perfect. You must not only see the head, but also the body, to see the person in his entirety. Yes, you may have seen Christ—that is wonderful. But you must realize that God's purpose not only involves the Head, but also His Body. You have seen

Christ, but for God's purpose you must also see the church. So the Lord Jesus said, "And I also say unto thee ..." You must underline, circle, and color the little word "also."

In all these years since we have seen something of the church, we cannot avoid telling others what we have seen. Because of this, we are accused of speaking too much about the church. Some dear friends say that they are for Christ. As long as they have Christ, say they, that is sufficient. They are always speaking about the Head. We too have seen the Head, but we have also seen the Body. We tell people that the Head is indeed important, the Head is precious, the Head is wonderful. But if you have only a head without a body, what kind of person is that? If we have only Christ without the church, what is that? Suppose that when we meet together the head of one of the brothers comes floating into the meeting hall. We would probably all flee in terror. The head needs the body. Oh, how much Christ needs the church! The problem is that people have talked much about the Head, but have neglected the Body. Some indeed have not only neglected the Body, but even opposed the Body and would stop others from speaking of it. So we must not only point others to the Head, but also to the Body. It is not only Christ, Christ, Christ, but also the church, the church, the church.

In other words, the Lord Jesus was saying to Peter, "It is wonderful that you have seen Christ, but you must see something more. And I say also unto you that I will build my church on what you have seen. You are Peter, a stone. I will build you with others as my church upon this rock. Henceforth you are no more an individualistic individual; you are just a stone built into the house, a member built into the Body. I will build my church—that means that I will build you as a stone with all the others as the church. This is the basis upon which I will give you the keys of the kingdom of heaven. You, Simon, are not worthy to have the keys. No, you are not qualified; but as a stone in the building, a member in the Body, you are positioned to have the keys of the kingdom of heaven." The revelation we must have is firstly of Christ, and secondly of the church.

It is indeed sad today that in Christianity so many refer to Matthew 16, but they always speak of Christ, not the church. We must see something of Christ and the church. The great mystery of God is Christ and the Church (Eph. 5:32). This is the revelation.

THE VISION

After a turn of time

The second portion begins with Matthew 17:1, "And after six days..." In the record of the same instance in Luke it says, "And it came to pass about eight days after these sayings..." (Luke 9:28). What is the difference? Really there is no difference. It was six full days. But according to the Jewish calendar you may also say it was eight days, including the last part of the first day and the first part of the last day. In any case, the meaning here is a period of one week—a week after the event referred to in chapter 16. A week is a specific turn of time, just as a full day is also a turn of time. A month and also a year with its four seasons are other turns of time. To see something of the Lord, we all need a turn of time. It does not depend upon you. Suppose that this morning you have missed the sun rising: you must wait for another turn of time, you must wait until the next morning before you will have another chance to see it. Suppose you have missed a sight of the full moon in these days: you cannot hope to see it within just a few days; you must wait until next month for another turn of time. Suppose you have missed the sight of the cherry trees blossoming this spring: you cannot hope to see such a sight in the summer, nor in the fall or winter; you must wait for another year, for another turn in time. To see something of the Lord, we all need to take advantage of the turn of time; we must not miss the opportunity. If in one meeting you do not see something of Him, you will have to wait until another meeting. If you miss the opportunity in one conference, you will have to wait for another conference. You need a turn of time. The times and the seasons are very meaningful. Be careful not to miss a day, a week, a month, or a year. Do not miss any opportunities. If you miss them, you must wait for another turn.

On the mountain top

Firstly the disciples saw the revelation, but they must wait a week, for another turn in time, before they could see something more. It was not up to them; it was up to the Creator of time. This time the Lord Jesus brought them to the mountain top, not only apart from all religious things and circumstances, but also apart from the earthly level. To see the revelation you must be far away from all religious things, persons, and circumstances; but to see the vision you must be on the mountain top, the higher the better. When we are on the mountain top, we get a clear view, we see the whole vision. It was there, not only apart from the religious circle, but also apart from earthly things, that Jesus became another Jesus. The Jesus you see on the mountain is not the Jesus you see at sea level. The Jesus on the mountain top is a transfigured Jesus. We need to be on the mountain top to see the vision, to see Jesus transfigured.

Jesus only

Many times while we are in a vision, however, some wonderful person breaks in. I cannot explain why, but I know the fact well. When Jesus was transfigured, while Peter, James and John were beholding Him, two wonderful persons entered upon the scene—Moses and Elijah. The whereabouts of Moses after his death, you remember, was a mystery. Following his death, God hid his body. No one knew where Moses was buried (Deut. 34:5-6). Then suddenly he appeared. While Jesus was transfigured, this mysterious person was manifested. Then there was another wonderful personality—Elijah. He also, in a sense, was a mystery. He was taken away in a chariot of God, no one knew where (2 Kings 2:11-12). Two wonderful, mysterious persons suddenly appeared.

Be careful! When you see a vision, many times Moses and Elijah will also appear. Why? I cannot explain it. In any case, be careful, be on the alert. Peter in the revelation was absolutely right and crystal clear, but now Peter in the vision is utterly frustrated. He was so frustrated that he began to talk nonsense again. Firstly he said, "Lord, it is good for us to be here." That is all right—just this much. It is really good for us to be with the Lord to see the vision—let us not say anything more. But Peter continued, "If thou wilt..." Peter was so religious—he would not do anything by himself, but always by the will of God. "If thou wilt, I will make here three tabernacles; one for thee, and one for Moses, and one for Elijah." He thought he was making a marvelous proposition. And what he was saying was certainly reasonable enough, religiously speaking. But while he was talking a cloud overshadowed them, and a voice out of the cloud shocked Peter: "This is my beloved Son, in whom I am well pleased; hear ye Him." God was saying, "Do not say that you will build one tabernacle for Moses and one for Elijah—there is only One in My sight. This is my beloved Son, hear ye Him." Because Jesus had come, there was no more Moses and no more Elijah as far as what they represented was concerned. Moses represented the law and Elijah represented the prophets. There was no more law and no more prophets, only the beloved Son of God. "Hear Him, Peter. Do not talk any more." Peter was shocked and fell to the earth sore afraid. Then they saw no man, save Jesus only. *No man, save Jesus only.*

Forgotten revelation

You may say that Peter was indeed too hasty. I do agree. However, Peter here in the vision was not just frustrated. What was more serious, he forgot two things: he forgot Christ, and he also forgot the church; he forgot the Head, and he also forgot the Body. He had already received the full revelation of Christ and the church, but now in the vision he was frustrated to such an extent that he forgot all about it. He forgot firstly about Christ as the Son of the living God. When he said, "I will make here three tabernacles: one for thee, one for Moses, and one for Elijah," he was lowering the level of Christ and uplifting the level of the other two persons to make them all equal. That means he forgot the revelation. Do you see this? Only Jesus is the Son of God. How can we put any wonderful and mysterious person on the same level as Christ? If we do that, we have forgotten the revelation of Christ the Head.

Secondly, Peter also forgot the revelation of the church, the revelation of the building. Jesus had said to Peter in effect, "You are a stone. I will build you up with others as the church. Henceforth, you should not behave individualistically. From now on, you must always realize that you are built up with others; you cannot act on your own." If Peter had really remembered the revelation of the church, he could never have spoken as he did. On the mountain, in the vision, Peter behaved in an outrageously individualistic way, forgetting all the other members. Jesus did not bring Peter alone to the mountain top; there were two others with him. But Peter forgot all about them. Peter forgot the revelation of Christ as the Head, and he also forgot the revelation of the church, including John and James. He did not behave in the Body; he behaved in himself.

Brothers and sisters, you may say, "Hallelujah! In the conference, or by reading a certain book, I have received the revelation of the Body. I have got it!" But, I tell you, when you get home, when you lay the book down, you will forget it. You will just behave in yourself; you will not have any Body sense, any Body feeling, any Body realization. When you think a certain course is right, you will just say so; when you consider a certain action to be good, you will just do it; you will never consider James and

John. The Lord has put you together with James and
John, but you do not care for them. You are so individualistic, and you are so accustomed to being individualistic.
In your past life you have always acted in this way. You
are a real Peter. How you behave on the mountain top
simply proves that you have forgotten the whole revelation
of Christ as the Head and the church as the Body.

The Lord gave Peter a lesson. The Lord was saying to
Peter, "You must remember that I am the Head, and that
you are just a stone builded into the house. You should
not be individualistic any more; you must go along with
others, not forgetting John and James. Do not act on your
own. Why do you have two brothers beside you and you
would not consult with them? Because you are so individualistic." We need the Head and we need the Body; we
need Christ and we need the church.

THE APPLICATION

The tribute men

God is sovereign: He can send some very wonderful
persons like Moses and Elijah, and He can also send some
troublesome people. In the last portion of these two
chapters we read, "And when they were come to Caper-
naum, they that received tribute money came to Peter"
(17:24). Tax collectors are troublesome people. But notice,
these tribute men are not the publicans; they are different.
The publicans were the tax gatherers for the Roman
Empire, for those who invaded Judea, occupied it and put
a heavy tax upon it. The tribute men in chapter 17 were
those who gathered taxes, not for the Roman Empire or
any other government, but for the maintenance of God's
house, the temple. God's people, the children of Israel,
were told in Exodus 30:11-16 that every male among them
must pay a half shekel to maintain God's house. God sent
such men to Peter.

God sent Moses and Elijah to appear in their vision,
but following the vision, in the application, God sent
another kind of person. If you do mean business with the

Lord, after you have seen the vision—be careful and be ready—God will send you some tribute men. Who will be the tribute men to you? Perhaps, firstly, your dear wife. Many times after we have received the vision, our dear wife comes just as a tribute man to collect something. You may exclaim, "Thank God, I'm not married! I do not have a wife, I do not have a husband: so there is no tribute man for God to send me." Then the first tribute man to come to you may be your roommate or your classmate. On the mountain top you see the vision, but when you get home, the tribute men arrive. In the conference, in the meeting. you receive the vision. You shout, Hallelujah! You are so happy with the vision. But when you get within the door of your home, the tribute men will be waiting for you. God is sovereign; He knows how to test you. Sometimes He uses our children, and many times He uses our in-laws as the tribute men. He can use anyone and everyone to put us on the test. We cannot avoid it; we cannot run away; the tribute men will find us. Every one of us has some tribute men.

Peter caught again

The tribute men came to Peter, and again Peter took the lead. All the rest of the disciples were in the house with Jesus, and Peter came out to meet and deal with the tribute men. Again he got caught. One who takes the lead always puts himself in a very dangerous position.

The tribute men said to Peter, "Doth not your Master pay tribute?" Brother Peter, do not forget what you learned in Matthew 16, Christ and the church—remember Peter? Do not forget the revelation you received. And secondly, Brother Peter, do not forget the lesson you learned so hard on the mountain top—Christ and His Body. But listen, when the test came Peter forgot everything. He forgot the revelation, he forgot the vision; he forgot Christ and the church, and He forgot the Head and the Body. He forgot everything; he only remembered himself. "Doth not your Master pay tribute?" "Yes," Peter immediately replied. Peter, how can you forget so quickly? Didn't you hear the voice on the mountain saying that you must "hear Him"? You must go to Him; you must ask Him; you should not answer yes or no. "Hear ye Him!" If we should speak in this way to Peter, Peter would argue, "Brother, you do not know the Bible. I can show you the chapter and verse telling us clearly that every male among the people of Israel must pay tribute, and Jesus is one of the males. Why shouldn't He pay? Surely it is right for me to say yes." Peter was very scriptural, very fundamental; Peter answered according to Moses' directions in Exodus 30. Peter answered the question according to the law—by listening to Moses and hearing him. But what he said was absolutely against his revelation, absolutely contrary to his vision and the heavenly voice, "Hear ye Him." There is no more Moses, no more law, no more Elijah, no more prophets—only Jesus; hear ye Him. Why after he had seen the vision did he keep his old knowledge, his tradition, and religion? This is the problem. After we see the vision, the old traditions, teachings and religion still hang on. "Doth not your Master pay tribute?" "Yes!" This "yes" comes from the old scriptural knowledge. It comes from the very teachings of the Bible. It is a right, scriptural, and fundamental answer. But it is one hundred percent against the vision, one hundred percent against Christ.

Peter then came into the house. I believe he returned with the intention of telling the Lord Jesus what he had done and to collect the money. But the Lord anticipated what he was going to say and forestalled him. The Lord was not about to let him talk any more. His implication was this: "Do not say that is scriptural, do not say that is fundamental; that is nonsense. Yes, that is according to your Bible, but not according to the living Christ, the present Christ."

Jesus is today's Moses

The Lord Jesus is really wise. Our speech is always so stupid, but the Lord Jesus always speaks in a very simple and pleasing tone. He did not rebuke Peter and tell him that he should not have said yes. The Lord was not so coarse, so rough as we are. He was outside of tradition and religion, but he was nicely outside of them. He asked Peter, "What thinkest thou Simon? The kings of the earth, from whom do they receive toll or tribute? from their sons, or from strangers?" (17:25). He spoke very nicely to Peter. Then Peter answered, "From strangers." The Lord Jesus replied, "Therefore the sons are free." He said in effect, "You have already heard on the mountain top that I am the Son of God; therefore, I am free from this tribute. This tribute is collected for my Father's house, and I am the Father's Son; so I am free."

Then Peter should have said something like this to the Lord: "Oh, I'm sorry, Lord; I should not have said 'yes,' I should have said 'no.' Anyhow, now what shall I do?" When Peter said yes, the Lord Jesus found a way to convince him that it should have been no. However, after Peter was convinced that he should have said no, Jesus said unto him, "But..." (v. 27). You can never beat the Lord Jesus in speaking. "But lest we cause them to stumble,...take, and give unto them for me and thee." When we say yes, the Lord says no, and then when we are convinced to say no, He says yes. The Lord is really troublesome. Eventually what is right and what is wrong? Should it be yes or should it be no? Eventually, there is no right or wrong, no yes or no—only Jesus! With the same case, when you say yes, he may say no, and when you say no, He may say yes. But whatever He says is right. "Hear ye Him!"—"Jesus only!" He is today's Moses; He is today's Lawgiver; He is the law today. There is no more Moses; there is only Jesus. Do not hear what the Old Testament says; hear Him. What would you say? In any case, whatever you say is wrong. Even if you are scriptural, you are still wrong; even if you are fundamental, you are still wrong. It is not a matter of being scriptural or fundamental, but a matter of Christ, a matter of the living, up-to-date, present Jesus. Everything depends on such a One. There is no law, no teaching, no regulations— only Jesus. And not a Jesus in doctrine but a Jesus who is so living, so instant, and so present.

Some young brothers have been greatly troubled over the matter of a haircut. How should they cut their hair? In what style? I will tell you, go to Jesus and ask Him. See what your living Jesus would say. There is no religion, no culture, no regulation, only Jesus.

In the summer of 1969 there was quite an influx of ex-hippies into the church in Los Angeles. They came in with long hair, long beards, sandals, and corresponding attire. Some brothers came to me at the time and said, "Brother. be careful, we might end up being a 'hippie' church." I answered them that I do not stand on either side: I am not for the hippies, and I am not against the hippies. Today it is not a matter of right or wrong, but absolutely a matter of the living, up-to-date Jesus. When He says, "Long hair!" then you may leave your hair long. When He says, "Short hair!" then you must cut your hair. When you go for a haircut, just say, "O Lord Jesus, how long?" Then you will know how long. Ask the Lord, "O Lord Jesus, what style?" Then you will know what style.

I would say a word in regard to the sisters and their skirts. I do not know how long is long and how short is short. You go to the presence of Jesus and ask Him. Jesus is within you; see what He says. You will know; the living Jesus will tell you. If you go to the sixty-six books of the Bible, there is not one verse to tell you how long your skirts should be. You must go to the living Jesus. Do not argue and reason—go to Jesus.

Some like to make laws for themselves, and some like to make laws for others. Immediately they become today's Moses. Do not make laws for yourselves, and do not make any laws for others. Hear ye Him!

When it came to the application, Peter not only forgot Christ, but also his brothers. When the tribute men came, if I were Peter and had learned my lesson, I would have called the Lord and my other brothers James and John and asked them to deal with the tribute men. Then I would have received the help I needed. You see, this is the Body life. Peter saw the vision, but Peter forgot the whole thing. With Peter there was no Christ, no Church, no Head, and no Body—only Peter himself. This is our problem. Today, in all our situations, we must remember our Head and also the members of the Body. Do not say yes or no, do not say anything, do not make any decisions until you have come to the Head and also to the Body. We are so accustomed to being individualistic.

Jesus gives Peter a lesson

In any case, by the Lord's talk with him, Peter was convinced and his mouth was shut. I do believe that Peter finally learned that he should never open his quick mouth and say yes or no, but let Jesus do the speaking. The lesson is not so easy. You must pay something for this lesson.

Then the Lord said to Peter, "Have you been convinced not to say yes or no? Then you go fishing. Go to the sea; there is no transportation, and I do not know how far you have to go. Just go fishing, and cast a hook into the water. Eventually you will catch a fish: open its mouth and find a coin which will be good not only for Me, but also for you, not only for the Head, but also for the Body." If I were Peter, I would be greatly distressed. I would say, "Lord, you want me to go fishing, all by myself? Aren't you going to send John or James with me?" But the Lord would answer, "No, I will not send them with you, because you do not need them. Even if I sent them, you would never listen to them. You always make the decisions yourself, so go fishing by yourself. Learn the lesson that you need your brothers. Go to the sea, cast the hook into the water, and wait until the first fish comes."

Peter went then to the sea and did as the Lord commanded. I simply cannot believe that he caught the fish immediately. I do believe the Lord made him wait awhile for the first fish to come, giving him plenty of time to consider what had just transpired. I can imagine him there with a line in the water, waiting and waiting, considering and considering. All the time the lesson was being driven into him deeper and deeper. Peter had a hard lesson to learn.

Christ is today's Elijah

At last Peter caught the fish just as the Lord had said. We must now see that the Lord is not only today's Moses, but also today's Elijah. He is not only the One Who gives the laws, but also the One who prophesies, who predicts. When He told Peter to go fishing, take the first fish and find in it a coin, this was a great prophecy. The illustration was rather small, but the implication is profound. Christ today is both Moses and Elijah: He gives the laws and He prophesies. When He predicts anything, it will certainly be fulfilled. There is no more Moses and no more Elijah; there is only Jesus—hear ye Him. Since we have Jesus, we need Moses no longer; since we have Jesus, we need Elijah no longer. He is the present Moses, and He is the present Elijah. Whatever He commands, that is the law; whatever He predicts, that is the prophecy.

Furthermore, with whatever the Lord commands He also prophesies the way whereby we may fulfill what He has commanded. This is indeed marvelous. Moses could only command; Moses could never afford anything in the way of supply for the people to fulfill his commandments. But the Lord is both the Commander and also the Fulfiller. Do you see this? The Lord not only gives us the commandments, but also affords us the supply to fulfill His commandments. What we need to do is just to go along with Him. When He says no, we must simply go along with Him and say no. When He says yes, we must go along with Him and say yes. When He says, "Go fishing," then we must go fishing; when He says, "Cast the hook into the water," just cast it into the water. When He says, "Wait until the fish comes," then just wait there until it comes. When He says, "Open the mouth of the fish," be simple, just open the mouth of the fish. When He says to take the coin from the fish's mouth, do it. Go along with His word, not merely with the word of the Bible, but the word of the living Jesus.

The living presence of the living Christ

We have seen that when Moses and Elijah appeared with the Lord on the mount, God, speaking from heaven, obviated them. God took away Moses and Elijah. In this sense, when the Lord comes, God takes away the Old Testament. When your dear ones are away from home, they send you photos and snapshots of themselves. That is what the Lord did in sending Moses and Elijah. But now our dear One is with us. Do we still need His pictures or letters? If we do, it means that we care more for them than for Himself. This would be an offense to Jesus. So many so-called fundamentalists today just care for reading the Bible; they do not care for the presence of Christ. They care for the letters, but they do not care for the living Christ. We have seen that Christ is versus religion. But now I have the boldness to say that, in a sense, Christ is also versus the Scriptures. What I mean is that Christ is versus the Scriptures as dead letters.

Brothers and sisters, you must see no man save Jesus only; you must hear Him, not the law nor the prophets, neither Moses nor Elijah. Jesus is today's Moses and He is the present Elijah. He is the Lawgiver, and He is the One who predicts. Go along with whatever He predicts, and you will have the ability to keep His commandments and fulfill what He says. Today's recovery is the recovery of the living presence of the living Christ, not the scriptural teachings, nor this or that. Whatever He says is right. Whatever He predicts will be fulfilled. Hallelujah!

Applying both Christ and the church

I really like the Lord's way. The Lord told Peter to go fishing and find a coin which would be good "for me and thee." The Lord took care not only of the Head, but also of the Body. He took care not only of Himself, but also of His members. Praise the Lord, the Head and the Body always go together.

Today we need the revelation, the vision, and even more the application that we may practice all that we have seen concerning Christ and the church, the Head and the Body. We must not only take care of the Head, but also of the Body. The coin was good for the Head and the Body. May the Lord show us more and more and bring us through not only the revelation and the vision, but also the application. When all the tribute men come to us, may we learn to apply both Christ and the church to our circumstances, not just in doctrine or teaching, but in practicality. The Lord be merciful and gracious to us all.

CHAPTER FIVE

WHAT THINK YE OF CHRIST?

Scripture Reading: Matt. 21:23-27, 37-39, 42-46: 22:1-4, 15-40, 41-46

THE EXAMINATION OF THE PASSOVER LAMB

In Matthew chapters 21 and 22 we have the fulfillment of a type in the Old Testament with which many are not familiar. Before the Passover, according to God's commandment, the people of Israel must prepare a lamb at least four days in advance (Exod. 12: 3, 6). During that period of preparation, the lamb was thoroughly examined for any spot or blemish. The lamb must be absolutely perfect to qualify for the Passover. We know that the Passover lamb was a type of the Lord Jesus Christ. He is the Lamb. Before He went to the cross to fulfill the Passover, He spent about six days in Jerusalem, and that through which He passed during these days was the fulfillment of the examination performed on the Passover lamb. During this time the people put Jesus on probation. Matthew 21 and 22 reveal the examination to which He was subjected. He was examined by leaders and representatives of all the current social, political, and religious parties. Let us see who they were.

First of all there were the chief priests and the elders of the people (21:23). The chief priests were those who held authority in religion; they were the ones who served God in the temple. The elders were those with authority among the people, the community. Thus, the first ones to examine Jesus were those with authority in religion and authority in the community—the chief priests and the elders. It was they who asked, "By what authority doest thou these things? And who gave thee this authority?" (21:23). The second examination was made by the Pharisees, the strongest religious party, together with the Herodians, a political party. Religion combined with politics (strange bedfellows) to put Jesus through the second examination. The third examination was performed by the Sadducees, the ancient modernists. In today's Christianity there are many who do not believe that Jesus is the Son of God, who died on the cross, shedding His blood for our redemption, and who was raised physically and literally from the dead. The modernists are today's Sadducees, and the Sadducees were the ancient modernists. They did not believe in the Word of God nor in the power of God; they did not believe in resurrection, or in angels or spirit (Acts 23:8). Lastly, in the fourth examination, one of the prominent Pharisees, a lawyer, put Jesus to the test.

Have you seen the picture? The chief priests and the elders among the people, the disciples of the Pharisees and the Herodians, the Sadducees, and then a lawyer, an expert among the Pharisees, all surrounded this little Jesus. All these learned people with the highest attainments, knowledge, position, names, and power combined to examine Christ and find some fault in Him. Jesus had never received a degree. He came from a despised town in a despised area and stood thus in the midst of these leaders. But praise the Lord, though He was small outwardly, He was not small inwardly. He had no pretentious form without, but He had tremendous power within. He had no outward knowledge, but He had infinite inward wisdom. He answered all the questions and He passed all the tests. He was put on probation and examination by so many leaders, and He passed through triumphantly.

Eventually, He put them to the test, and by one stone He killed all the birds. By one question He shut all their mouths. They put Jesus to the test four times, and the Lord Jesus put them to the test once. By all these questions, four plus one, we may see how very much Christ was versus religion.

THE FIRST QUESTION

The high priest, the authority of the religion, and the elders, the authority of the community, combined together to raise the first question, a question concerning the source of Jesus' authority. "By what authority doest thou these things? And who gave thee this authority?" (21:23). In other words, they asked, "What is your source? Is your authority authentic? Where did a little man like you get this authority?" We should not consider such questions lightly. In Christianity today people are always asking such questions: "What about his origin? Is that fundamental? Is that sound?" What they really mean, and sometimes they say it in so many words, is this: "From what seminary has he graduated? Where was he ordained, and by whom was he ordained?"

The Lord Jesus, of course, was so wise. He said, "I also will ask you one question, which if ye tell me, I likewise will tell you by what authority I do these things. The baptism of John, whence was it? From heaven or from men?" (21:24-25). He really put them on the spot. Then those learned ones with the highest attainments reasoned among themselves saying, "If we shall say, From heaven; he will say unto us, Why then did ye not believe him?" (21:25). What they meant was that if they endorsed John, they would have to receive Jesus, because John testified of Him and was His forerunner. If they accepted John, they must also accept Jesus. Thus, they said in effect, "We cannot say that. If we do, we will fall into a trap." Then they said, "But if we shall say, From men; we fear the multitude, for all hold John as a prophet" (21:26). Eventually they decided that the best solution would be to tell a lie. So they turned back to Jesus and said, "We know not." But the Lord Jesus knew that they knew. He said in effect, "You know, but you won't tell Me. You say you don't know, but that is a lie. The truth is that you won't tell Me. And since you won't tell Me, neither will I tell you. You lie, but I will not lie." Jesus is really Lord. He is really worthy of our worship. Who could answer a question in this way but Jesus?

Following this answer of the Lord to the chief priests and elders of the people, He proceeded to speak to them in parables. I will just refer briefly to the last two. In the second parable the Lord indicated that He was there for God's building (21:33-46). They had spoken to Him in a foolish and sinful way, but in spite of that the Lord Jesus proceeded to unveil something of God's revelation, of God's eternal purpose. In this parable He indicated first that He is the Son of God. God sent His Son unto them, and this Son is the heir who will receive all God's inheritance. What they were doing was rejecting this heavenly and divine heir, the Son of God. Secondly, the Lord Jesus told them that in rejecting such a One, they were rejecting the very cornerstone for God's building. He said in other words, "You do not know what you are talking about. You do not know what you are doing. You do not know whom you are rejecting. I am here as the Son of God, rejected by you; but eventually what you reject will become the headstone of the corner." For what purpose? For God's building. Even in the Lord's answer to such foolish ones, He indicated that He was for God's building.

Following this, He spoke the parable of the wedding feast (22:1-14). The Son of God is the cornerstone, and the Son of God is also the Bridegroom. Thus, the Lord revealed two marvelous things—the building and the wedding feast. The building requires the feast, and the feast is for the building. The more we feast upon Jesus, the more we will be built into His building. The Lord's answer in these parables is so full of meaning. By referring to I Corinthians 3 and I Peter 2, we see that the feasting is for the growth, and the growth is for the building. Therefore, we all must feast at the wedding feast of Jesus that we may grow, and as we grow we will become proper material for the building. He is the chief cornerstone for the building, and we are the many stones. We become the stones by feasting on Him. God's intention with the Lord Jesus is simply the building and the feast, the enjoyment and the building up.

THE SECOND QUESTION

Then the Pharisees realized it was not so easy to defeat such a One; so they asked the Herodians to join them. The Pharisees were not only the religious party, but also a patriotic party, faithful to the Jewish nation. They were patriotic as well as religious; they loved their country and were eager to protect it. At that time their nation was under the rule of the Roman empire—to the Pharisees, a detestable situation. The Herodians, on the other hand, were the very representatives of this imperialistic domination. How could two such parties, the Pharisees and the Herodians, ever work together? They could because they had a common enemy. They came together to put Jesus on the spot by entangling Him in His words. They asked, "What thinkest thou? Is it lawful to give tribute unto Caesar, or not?" (22:17). This tribute differed from that in Matthew 17. This was a tax paid to the Roman government. All the faithful, patriotic Jews in ancient times were against this—they would never pay one penny if they could help it. Thus they thought they could certainly catch Jesus by putting Him on the horns of a dilemma. Their question was very subtle. If Jesus should answer that it was not lawful to give tribute to Caesar, then the Herodians would immediately pounce upon Him, accusing Him of opposition to the Roman empire. However, if on the other hand He should say that it was lawful for the Jews to pay the Roman tax, the patriotic party of the Jews would reply, "This man is betraying our country." Such was the subtlety of the Pharisees.

Do you think there was no way for the Lord Jesus to escape? Do you think that anyone could entangle Him? No, even if ten parties combined together against Him, they still could not succeed. He has a way. Hallelujah, He is Jesus! Notice what He did. The wisest thing was that

He did not take the tribute money out of His own pocket. He said to them, "Show me the tribute money." And they brought unto Him a denarius (22:19). They brought the tribute money—that means that they had already lost the case. They came to Jesus asking whether or not tribute should be paid to Caesar, but they had Roman money, not Jesus. They lost their case. They had the Roman money, and they kept the Roman money; so they were caught. Jesus is the Lord! Don't try to arrest Jesus; if you do, you will be arrested by Him.

Then He asked them, "Whose is this image and superscription?" They said unto Him, "Caesar's." The Lord Jesus answered, "Render therefore unto Caesar the things that are Caesar's." But He did not stop there. He left no ground for the enemy. He went on to add, "And unto God the things that are God's" (22:20-21). Their mouths were shut. When they heard this, they marveled at His answer.

THE THIRD QUESTION

Following this the Sadducees, the ancient modernists, took their turn. They thought they were more clever and could ensnare Jesus. They said in effect, "Master, there are some who believe in resurrection, but we have a problem. According to the regulation of Moses' law, if a man die, having no children, his brother shall marry his wife and raise up seed unto his brother. Now there were with us seven brethren, and the first married and died, and having no seed left his wife unto his brother. The second brother did likewise, and the third, unto the seventh. And after them all, the woman died. In the resurrection, therefore, whose wife shall she be of the seven?" They really thought they were smart. The Lord Jesus answered, "Ye do err, not knowing the scriptures, nor the power of God" (22:29). The Lord Jesus rebuked them in His answer. He said in effect, "You don't know the Bible. You thought you knew, but really you don't. You don't know the Bible; neither do you know the power of

God." He went on then to say, "For in the resurrection they neither marry, nor are given in marriage...But as touching the resurrection of the dead, have ye not read that which was spoken unto you by God saying, I am the God of Abraham, and the God of Isaac, and the God of Jacob? God is not the God of the dead, but of the living" (22:30-32). Jesus was saying to them, "All these people— Abraham, Isaac, and Jacob—are dead; if they are not resurrected, then God would be a God of the dead. But God could never be the God of the dead; He is the God of the living. This proves that they will all be living, they will be resurrected. You Sadducees know the letter of this title—the God of Abraham, the God of Isaac, and the God of Jacob—but you do not know the reality in it. The letter of the Word informs you that God is the God of these three persons. But the reality in this title is that there will be a resurrection. This title proves that God will resurrect these three persons; otherwise, He would be the God of the dead instead of the living."

These modernistic Jews in ancient times attempted to corner Jesus. But Jesus took this opportunity to show how they needed to know the Scriptures in a living way, how they needed to know the power of God, and how they needed to know that God is the living God. Since God is living, His people too should be living. We too must know the Scriptures in a living way, we too must know the power of God, and we too must be the living people to know the living God. They were astonished, and they lost their case.

THE FOURTH QUESTION

Then the Pharisees, when they heard that the Sadducees were put to silence, attempted again to examine Jesus. One of them, a lawyer, asked Him a question, trying Him: "Teacher, which is the great commandment in the law?" (22:36). He asked in other words, "How do you expound the Books of Moses?" This question concerned the exposition and interpretation of the Bible. It was exceedingly easy, of course, for the Lord Jesus to deal with this. He replied, "Thou shalt love the Lord thy God with all thy heart, with all thy soul, and with all thy mind. This is the great and first commandment. And the second like unto it is this, Thou shalt love thy neighbor as thyself" (22:37-39). It is so simple. The law and the prophets all hang on these two commandments. The Lord gave them the proper answer. Then they had no word to say. Eventually all their mouths were shut. But they would not depart; they still continued there to lose the case.

Just consider: besides these four kinds of problems, what other questions could be raised? The first related to religion, the second to politics, the third to the faith, and the fourth to scriptural interpretation. Today in Christianity we still have all these problems, and people pay their full attention to them.

THE LORD'S QUESTION

To all these questions, the Lord Jesus undoubtedly had an answer. But now the Lord Himself raised a question. I would call this the question of questions. "Now while the Pharisees were gathered together, Jesus asked them a question, saying, What think ye of the Christ? Whose Son is He?" (22:41-42). Today, in the entire universe, it is not a matter of religion, politics, the faith, or the interpretation of the Scriptures, but altogether a matter of Christ. What do you think of Christ? Who is He? It is so simple. Christianity today deals with all these matters—religion, politics, faith, and scriptural interpretation—but hardly a one will deal with the living Christ. They tackle every matter but the living Christ Himself. We are in exactly the same situation today as in the ancient times.

The Pharisees answered Jesus rightly. They replied that Christ is the Son of David. But then Jesus asked in effect, "How then could David, the grandfather, call the grandson his Lord?" That shut their mouth. They could

answer in the way of knowledge, but they could not
discern reality in the Spirit. They had learned that Christ
is the Son of David, but they had received no revelation
in the spirit that this Christ who is on one hand the Son
of David is also the Lord of all. They were one hundred
percent in their mind and not one percent in their spirit.
They had the Bible, but they missed Christ. How many
dear ones have been distracted, frustrated, and kept away
from Christ by Bible knowledge. This does not mean that
we do not need the Bible. We need it, but we need it in
a spiritual way, a living way. We must be careful never
to let Bible knowledge blind us to the living Christ. It is
not a matter of knowledge or teaching, but absolutely a
matter of the living Christ. It is His living presence, it
is His living Spirit. The letter kills, the knowledge
deadens, and scriptural interpretation confuses, frustrates
and distracts. We need the living Bible, the living Word,
the living teaching. If so, we must turn ourselves from
our mind to the spirit and learn like David to be in spirit
to call Him Lord. "O Lord! O Lord! O Lord! I do not care
for my knowledge, I do not care for any teaching, I just
care for my living Lord in my spirit. I turn to my spirit
and call Him Lord." By your mental figuration, you can
never understand the Bible. If you would see something
of this book, you must virtually cut off your head and
turn yourself wholly and thoroughly to your spirit and
say, O Lord!

Religion, politics, the faith, and scriptural interpretation must all pass away for us. Christ has the answer to
each of these questions, but He does not care for them;
neither must we care for anything but the living Lord,
the living Christ. As long as we have His presence, it is
sufficient. We must learn just to turn to our spirit and
say, O Lord! This is the way to experience Him.

We must all realize the Lord's marvelous wisdom in
questioning the Pharisees. In His question the Lord
referred to the matter of His person. This is a tremendous
matter. If we would know the Lord, we must know His

person. On the one hand He is the Son of man, but on the other hand He is also the Son of God. As the Son of man He is a descendant of David, but as the Son of God He is the Lord today. As the Son of man He is a real man, but as the Son of God He is God Himself. We must all realize the two natures of the Lord's person. He is divine as well as human; He is a human being as well as a divine person. The question He directed to the Pharisees indicates all the things related to Him.

THE ASCENDED CHRIST

But the Lord Jesus not only asked a question. He went on to quote Psalm 110, verse 1, where God is recorded as saying to Christ, "Sit thou on my right hand, till I put thine enemies underneath thy feet." It is abundantly clear that this refers to the ascension of Christ. Don't care for any religion, don't be concerned that much with politics, don't labor so much over the so-called Christian faith, and don't pay so much attention to scriptural interpretation. We must all concentrate upon Christ as the exalted and ascended One. The ascension of the Lord Jesus is the climax of all that He is, of all that He has done, and of all that He will do. Consider the chart on the opposite page. Christ in the beginning was the Word, and the Word was God. Then He was incarnated; He passed through human life on this earth; He was put into death, buried, and resurrected. He passed through all these things and ascended to the peak of the universe. After His ascension, He came down in another way with another form. He descended not only as the Spirit of life, but also as the Spirit of power. As such a One He is building the church and preparing it as His Bride for His second coming, at which time He will usher in the millennium, the kingdom. And one day He with all He has accomplished and gained will be in eternity as God and the Lamb with the New Jerusalem. The Lord in Matthew 22:41-45 is referring not only to Himself as a person, but as a person in ascension. He is the ascended One. In this passage He is at the

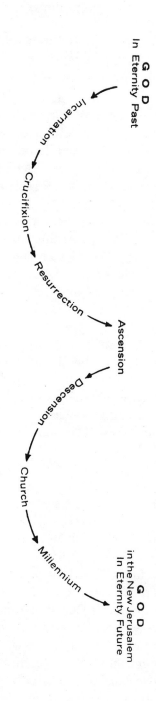

THE ASCENSION CLIMAX OF CHRIST

G O D
In Eternity Past

Incarnation

Crucifixion

Resurrection

Ascension

Descension

Church

Millennium

G O D
in the New Jerusalem
In Eternity Future

climax, the peak. As the ascended One, He includes everything from eternity past to His ascension and everything from His ascension to eternity in the future. Hallelujah for such an ascended Christ!

Today's Christians talk much about being saved. Then they are always complaining how poor or how weak they are. A few, on the other hand, say that by God's mercy they are not so weak, but indeed rather spiritual. But my burden is that we must be rescued from all these things. Forget about all these religious problems, politics, the so-called faith, and even the interpretation of the Bible. You talk so much regarding how to interpret and understand the Bible, but Jesus would ask, "What think ye of Christ?" There is a proper answer to all problems, but the main problem is, What think ye of Christ? Have you ever turned yourself from the Bible to the living, ascended Christ? Christians today pay so much attention to all other things, but nearly all neglect a continual living relationship with the living person of Christ. It is not principally, for example, a matter of whether you as a sister should wear a short or a long skirt. The vital point is what you think of Christ. It is absolutely a matter of Christ. Don't measure your skirt by the length, but by Christ. It must be a skirt of Christ. Whenever you speak about clothing, do not judge it by measurement, color, or style, but by Christ.

The best way to interpret the Bible is by Christ. The best way to care for the faith is by Christ. If you have Christ, surely you will have the proper faith. If you lack the living Christ, regardless of the creed you have, that is not the faith, that is a pity. We must care for nothing but Christ. We must even forget our Bible if we take it as a Bible without Christ. We need to forget our kind of faith—the sound, fundamental, scriptural faith—if it is a faith without a living touch with the living Christ. The Lord's intention is that we care only for Christ and the church. The Lord Jesus in answering all these ridiculous and foolish questions did not forget the church. We have already seen how He referred to the building of God, that is, the church. In His answer to all these questions He brings the questioners back to the matter of Himself and His church.

Thank the Lord that in these recent years so many have been rescued and delivered to a certain extent from religion. Yet we still have a certain amount of religion within us. By all these verses we may see that the Lord Jesus has nothing in His mind and heart but Himself and His church. We have been greatly distracted from Christ and the church by so many religious things, political things, matters concerning the sound faith and how to interpret the Bible. Years ago, the interpretation of the Bible was my favorite occupation and a real temptation. When a person came to me with one verse, I would expound fifty to him. But if you come to me today with a verse, I will reduce your verse to nothing but the living Christ. Forget about the interpretation of the Bible.

Sometimes the dear saints ask when the Lord Jesus will return. All I can answer is simply that He will return. Sometimes they ask what the signs of His coming are. All I can say is that the signs are simply the signs. Would you be willing to forget about all this and care only for the living Christ? Whether He comes today or tomorrow, with this sign or with that sign, it matters little. Just care for Christ; then you will be ready for His coming. Whenever a person asks concerning any matter, I would eventually say, "What think ye of Christ?"

Look at Christ today. He is the exalted One! Hallelujah! He was God in the beginning, who was incarnated and passed through all the human living on this earth. He experienced crucifixion and resurrection and was raised to the peak of the universe in ascension. Now, after His ascension, He is here as the Spirit of life and power, moving on this earth to establish His churches. He is the Son of man walking in the midst of all the local lampstands. He is here among us. This is the very thing for which we must care. He cares for the growth in number in the local churches, and He cares even more for the growth in life. He would say to us, "Do not be foolish like the chief priests, elders, Pharisees, Herodians, and Sadducees. Forget all the things they cared for, and concentrate on Christ and the church." If we don't understand some passage of the Bible, we simply don't understand it. We don't care for the mere understanding of the Bible. If we don't know what portion or chapter is the greatest in the Bible, we simply don't know. We don't care merely for knowing that. But we know that Christ is there and Christ is within us and Christ is among us. Oh, we care for the ascended Christ! He is not only the Son of man, but also the Son of God. He is not only the seed of David, but also the root of David. Why is it then that in the local churches we are dealing with the Bible all the time, we are pray-reading the Bible continually? Not merely for learning or understanding anything, but for eating Christ.

Yet in our meetings there is still some element of religion. Why are we so careful about keeping a certain kind of good order? It is because we are still religious. You may argue that the Apostle Paul tells us to do everything decently and in order. But the very fact that you mention this exposes the religion in you. Try your best to understand. I would like to hear and see you speak freely in your meetings about nothing but Christ and the church. Just come to the meeting in the spirit and feel free to say something about Christ. Feel free to present Christ. Feel free to minister Christ. Just feel free—don't be so careful. Some of you have been careful for years. I am afraid that at least a few of your hairs have turned gray by being careful in the meeting. Would you be willing to forget about being careful and just be free with Christ? Come into the meeting and be free with Christ, not in a sloppy way, but livingly in the spirit.

If you read through the entire Book of Matthew you will see that the Lord Jesus, while He was on earth, was not once careful concerning the Jewish religion. From the time He came to be baptized by John the Baptist He cared nothing for it nor was He ever careful concerning religious sensibilities. On the contrary, He always acted in human eyes so roughly and wrongly. He did it purposely to impress His disciples never to care for anything religious, but only for Christ and His church. I would advise you to read and to pray-read chapters 21 and 22 of Matthew five times. You will see how the Lord Jesus was absolutely outside of religion. He cared only for Himself and His building, the church.

CHAPTER SIX

THE PRESENCE OF
THE RESURRECTED CHRIST

Scripture Reading: Matthew 28

We have seen that the Book of Matthew is clearly a book concerning Christ versus religion. Now we come to the last chapter of this book. It is not a long chapter—indeed it is rather short—but its entire record is full of the contrast between Christ and religion. From the beginning to the end we may see the difference and the distance between Christ and religion.

In verse one we read, "In the end of the sabbath..." (King James Version). The sabbath, we know, was the symbol of the old Jewish religion. Therefore, when we read "In the end of the sabbath," it means at the end of the old religion. Hallelujah! The resurrection of Christ is the end of the old religion. A new age has dawned, the age of the resurrected Christ, not the old age of the old religion. We read further, "As it began to dawn toward the first day of the week..." Something was dawning—it was the resurrection of Christ. Something ended and something began.

THE AGE OF WOMEN

Now notice that it was Mary Magdalene and the other Mary who came to see the sepulchre. There is much significance, we know, in whatever the Bible says. We must realize that in the Old Testament every great event was always revealed to men, not to women. It is rather difficult to find one case in the Old Testament where God revealed anything firstly to a woman. In the Old Testament women were not reckoned. But here we read that the new start of the new age was discovered not by men, but by women. And all the women here were of the same name—Mary. There were no males—just females. This was against the old way, against the religious regulation. The old way was always with the men, but the new way is always with the women. I hope that the brothers will say, Hallelujah!

Let me check with you all, especially the brothers. Are you male or female? Today in the new age we must answer, spiritually speaking, that we are all females, we are all Marys. This is the vision; this is the new beginning.

It is not a small thing to discover the resurrection of Christ. We must be clear that the resurrection had occurred already, but before the women went there it was not discovered. In the end of chapter 27 we read that the chief priests and Pharisees sealed the grave with a stone and set a watch. But they never witnessed the resurrection. The stone was still there, but Jesus was gone. Apparently nothing had happened. Nobody knew that Jesus was resurrected, but by the coming of these Marys it was discovered. We read that there was a great earthquake and an angel of the Lord descended from heaven and rolled away the stone (v. 2). Why did he roll away the stone? To let Jesus out? No! It was to show the sisters that the tomb was empty.

The Lord's way today is not according to the old way. The age has changed. His resurrection was not discovered by men, but by women. Spiritually speaking, this is not the age of men, but the age of women. According to religion everything must be revealed to men; but here is something discovered by women. This is entirely contrary to religion.

THE MOUNTAIN IN GALILEE

The angels then told the women, "Go quickly, and tell his disciples, he is risen from the dead; and lo, he goeth before you into Galilee; there shall ye see him" (28:7). At that time all the disciples were at Jerusalem. Apparently, it would be more convenient for them to meet the Lord

right there. Why would the Lord go before His disciples
into Galilee? Physically and logically we can find no
reason. But I do believe the Lord Jesus did this deliberately and intention ally to impress His disciples that this
was a new start, that this new age has nothing to do with
the old religion. The Lord Jesus was saying in effect to
His disciples, "You must get out of that whole realm."
Eventually we will see how the poor disciples brought
things back to Jerusalem and to the temple (Acts 21:20-
26). Undoubtedly the Lord intended to impress His
disciples that everything related to Him is separate from
the old religion. He, the resurrected Christ, had nothing
to do with that religion and neither should they, His
disciples.

We must remember that the New Testament began
from Galilee. Jesus was conceived by His mother Mary,
not in Jerusalem, but in Galilee (Luke 1:26-38). It began
in Galilee, and it must be continued in Galilee. The angels
told the women, "He goeth before you into Galilee." Then
as they ran from the tomb with fear and great joy, Jesus
Himself met with them and said, "Go tell my brethren
that they depart into Galilee, and there shall they see
me" (v. 10).

Later in the chapter (v. 16) we see that it was not a
synagogue to which they were directed in Galilee, but to
a mountain in the open air. It was absolutely contradictory
to the religious concept. At that time all the religious
people either gathered in the temple at Jerusalem or in
the synagogues in the various other cities. But now Jesus
instructed His disciples to depart from Jerusalem and
thus from the temple. Then, when they went to Galilee,
He did not lead them into a synagogue or even into a
house, but to a mountain. Don't imagine that He did these
things without a purpose. We must believe that this is
full of significance. He did it to impress His disciples that
henceforth in the new age with the resurrected Christ
and His Body, the church, everything must be different
from religion. If religion goes to the north, then the church
must go to the south. If religion meets in the daytime,

then the church must meet at night. Christ and the church are always versus religion. At the present time we meet together on Sunday simply because people are free from their jobs on that day. If they could be free at some other time, I would say that it would be much better to meet on Friday or any other week day and forget about meeting on Sunday. This matter of Sunday worship is too much of religion. When religious people meet on Sundays, if possible, we would go to work. When they work, we would stop working and meet. I tell you, this was the principle adopted by the Lord Jesus. He said in effect, "You priests, you religious people, all go up to Jerusalem. You meet there, but I tell my disciples to go away to Galilee. You meet in the synagogue, but I tell my disciples to meet on the mountain top." Oh, Christ is really versus religion!

THE LORD'S BROTHERS

Jesus said to the women, "Go tell my brethren" (v. 10). This is a new term—"my brethren." Religious people always consider that we are at most the servants of the Lord, or to use a more intimate term, the children of the Lord. But the, Lord Jesus Himself referred to us as His brethren. This is a feature of the new age. Jesus is our Brother, and we are His brethren. That day they were going to meet their Brother. They were not going, in a sense, to meet their Lord and Master, but their very Brother. Have you ever praised the Lord in this way? Have you ever said, "Lord, how we praise You that You are our Brother"? I fear that if you go into any kind of Christian service today and praise the Lord Jesus in this way, you will be promptly quenched and charged with irreverence. Hallelujah, Jesus called us His brethren! He has the life of the Father, and we too have the life of the Father. We are no more just His disciples, no more merely His servants, but His very brothers. What He is, we are; and what we are, He is. He is the Son of God, and we are the sons of God. He is our Brother, and we are His brethren. We are going to the brothers' meetings. It is really good.

CHRIST VERSUS MONEY

Immediately after the discovery of the resurrected Christ, those religious people exercised their power. "Behold, some of the guard came into the city, and told unto the chief priests all the things that were come to pass. And when they were assembled with the elders, and had taken counsel, they gave much money unto the soldiers, saying, Say ye, His disciples came by night, and stole him away while we slept. And if this come to the governor's ears, we will persuade him, and rid you of care. So they took the money, and did as they were taught..." (vv. 11-15). By money and with money you can do everything. They exercised their power to bribe the people. Money is the power of today's religion. But notice what the Lord Jesus said to His disciples. He did not say, "All gold and silver have been given into my hand. Go ye therefore!" He did not say, "Those religious people have a lot of money. but I have more." No! He said, "All authority hath been given unto me in heaven and on earth. Go ye therefore..." (vv. 18-19). He said in effect, "Go with this. Don't go with money. Go with my authority." What a shame that in today's Christianity so many talk continually of money. Day by day on the radio, at the close of every religious broadcast, there is a plea for money. Christ is versus religion. Christ is versus money. Christ does not care for money, and neither should His church.

A THREE-VERSE CONFERENCE

Naturally and religiously speaking, we would think that if the Lord Jesus would have a meeting on the mountain in Galilee following His resurrection, that meeting must be a considerably long meeting with a message covering several chapters in the Bible. After His resurrection, we know, He was going to ascend to the heavens, and we would think that He must pass on many instructions and regulations for His disciples to follow in His absence. We may think that He should dictate to them the charters, creeds, doctrinal statements, conditions for

appointing elders and selecting deacons, and how to set
up the local churches, etc., etc. I would think the Lord
Jesus would need to schedule a three-week conference
with His disciples. But to our amazement, instead of a
three-week conference, there is a three-verse conference,
and it is recorded in Matthew 28:18-20. "Jesus came to
them and spake unto them, saying, All authority hath
been given unto me in heaven and on earth. Go ye
therefore, and make disciples of all the nations, baptizing
them into the name of the Father and of the Son and of
the Holy Spirit: teaching them to observe all things
whatsoever I commanded you: and lo, I am with you all
the days, even unto the completion of the age" (Greek).
This was the first conference following the resurrection
of Christ. This was the first church conference.

PUTTING PEOPLE INTO GOD

The Lord Jesus was so simple. Concerning the work
of the Lord He said simply, "Go ye therefore, and make
disciples of all nations, baptizing them into the name of
the Father and of the Son and of the Holy Spirit." That
is all. Our work must be like this. We must simplify our
work as much as possible. We must focus in our work
upon this one point—putting people into the triune God.
This is the meaning of the word "baptize." It means to
put people into something. To baptize them with water
means to put them into the water. Likewise, what we
must do today is simply to put people into the triune God.
Our work today should be so simple. Regardless of what
teaching or message we use, as long as people are put
into the triune God, that is quite sufficient. Christianity
performs a multitude of activities, but they keep people
outside of God. They speak about the triune God, but the
end product is that people never get into Him. Our job
today is just to bring people into God, to put people into
God.

THE LORD'S AUTHORITY AND PRESENCE

Why was this conference so short? Because of the

Lord's presence. He said, "Lo, I am with you all the days." There was no need for Him to tell them so many things. Whatever they needed the next day, He would let them know. And whatever they needed the day after that, He would also let them know. Whatever they needed in the first century, He was with them to tell them. And whatever they needed in the second century, He was also with them to tell them. There was no need for Him to dictate many things in detail. His presence is everything. He said to them in effect, "My authority is better than money, and my presence is better than all kinds of creeds and regulations."

Many people in the past have asked us concerning two things. One is the matter of money. "In what way do you raise funds? Please tell us the secret. Do you have someone backing you in your work? Are there some millionaires supporting you?" I have replied, "We have many backing us—many poor people. We have very few who are rich." When they insist on knowing where the money comes from, I can only answer, "You don't know, and I don't know either. I never learned how to raise money. We never even talk about it." Then they speak about the second matter: "We know that you don't have any organization, but you must have some kind of regulations and rules. What are they?" But the fact is we don't have any regulations and rules. These two things are in the religious mind all the time—how to raise money, and how to formulate a creed in writing. But here the Lord Jesus also mentions two things: 1) All authority is given unto Him. We must go forth with His authority. 2) He is with us all the days until the completion of this age. That is sufficient. What we have today are: 1) the authority of Jesus, and 2) the presence of Jesus. Hallelujah! We don't have financial resources and we don't have creeds, but we have something much better—the Lord's authority and the Lord's very presence.

I want to tell you today that I appreciate the presence of the Lord Jesus much more than the Bible. In the early years after I was saved I cannot tell you how much I loved my Bible. I loved that Book dearly, but I must honestly say that at that time I had little appreciation of the Lord's presence. I appreciated His Word, the Bible, but I did not so greatly appreciate His presence. l must tell you that today I still appreciate the Bible. In fact I must say that I appreciate it even more than I did in those first seven years. But I appreciate much more the living presence of the living Lord. He said, "Lo, I am with you all the days." That is good enough. That is wonderfully sufficient. What else could we want? What else do we need but the authority of the Lord and the presence of the living Christ?

In the new move of the Lord in this new age there is no regulation, organization, or creed. Forget about that! The Lord never even said that we must keep all the commandments of the Old Testament. He only said that we must teach the people what He has commanded us in a living way. We must say again that in this new age with the Lord's new move, there is no need of any kind of organization, system, or regulation. What we need is altogether dependent upon the Lord's presence. "Lo, I am with you all the days."

APPLYING THE LORD'S PRESENCE

We must be practical in applying this to our present situation. When the young people have their special meetings, they like to consider the way and format of their meeting. Many times they will come to the leading brothers asking for directions and fellowship as to how they must meet. In a sense this is good, but in another sense it is not. They must realize that the Lord is with them. They need only proceed to meet with the present Christ, the living Lord. He will show them how to meet. When they come into His presence, He will lead them and reveal to them moment by moment how to go on. It is really difficult for people to believe that there has ever been such a group of believers meeting in this way on this earth. You see, we are still rather religious even when we come together to meet. We always have the concept that we must know beforehand how we are going to meet. When we come to the meeting we are not so open to the living Jesus, the present Christ. We still retain certain religious concepts concerning how to meet.

When we read the record in this chapter of what the Lord said and did, we cannot find even a hint of anything religious. If we compare the record of this chapter with all the records of the Old Testament, there is a great contrast and difference. Not one matter resembles that which was spoken and performed in the Old Testament. Everything is changed; everything is new. We must realize and admit that in our concepts we still preserve the tenets of religion. If we were there, we would say to the Lord Jesus, "Please stay with us for another four weeks. We have so many questions; we have so many matters which require a solution. We don't know how to go on. You have told us to go and disciple the nations, but you have not told us: 1) Where? 2) When? 3) Who? 4) How? or 5) What? O Lord Jesus, please stay with us. Make everything clear." Be honest. Would we not speak in such a way?

In the past eight years many have come to me with these same questions: What? Where? When? Who? How? My answer all the time was, "I don't know. Look to the Lord. The Lord knows." Has the Lord not told us that He will be with us all the days? What else do we want? Why should anyone say to the Lord, "Don't go, Lord!" He never has gone and He never will—He is with us all the days.

Christians today believe that the Lord Jesus was resurrected, and they also believe that He ascended to heaven. But there are some who tell Him, "Lord, you stay there in the third heaven. Don't come down to interfere. You be the exalted Lord there, and let us do a good job for you here." So many behave in this way, leaving the Lord in heaven. When they encounter any problems, they fast and pray, asking the Lord to do something for them. But this is not the right way to go on. We must enjoy the Lord's presence continually. Whenever we face a difficulty, we need only turn to Him saying, "O Lord Jesus, this is not our problem, this is Your problem. You are here. If You can go to sleep, then we can do the same."

In this Book of Matthew, a book concerning Christ versus religion, it is indeed impressive and meaningful that the ascension of Jesus is never mentioned. There is not one verse or word in this book telling us that He ascended to the heavens. This book is a book of Emmanuel, God with us (Matt. 1:23). How could He ascend to the heavens? He is with us! It is this book which also says, "Where two or three are gathered together in my name, there am I in the midst of them" (18:20). "Lo, I am with you all the days, even unto the completion of the age." The church needs a present Christ. We believe that the Lord is undoubtedly in the heavens—Hallelujah! But today, He as the resurrected and living Christ is continually in the church with us. He is so wonderfully and really present. When we come together we do have the sense that while we are meeting He is here. We need this realization in all our meetings. We do not look to Him only as the ascended One, but as the present One. Hallelujah! Jesus is here!

Whenever I hear people speaking about Easter and saying that they will have a sunrise service, I always remark that every day to me is Easter and all our meetings are sunrise meetings. Every meeting is a celebration of the resurrected Christ. What day is it today? If it is Tuesday, then it must be Easter Tuesday. Every day should be Easter to us. Every meeting, whether it is in the morning or in the evening, must be a sunrise meeting. We should never have anything as a sunset, for we have the presence of the resurrected Christ!

Christians, especially in this country, are always asking where our headquarters are located. I would tell them now that if we have any headquarters, they are on the mountain top of Galilee. Our headquarters are with the resurrected Christ on the mountain top. We have nothing religious. All we have is the resurrected Christ. How much we all need to be delivered from the concept of religion! How much we have been poisoned with religious concepts, and how many religious concepts there are still in our blood! If you will pray-read all these verses, bring all these points to the Lord and put them into practical application, you will see how much you still need the deliverance of the Lord.

In conclusion what we have today is just the resurrected Christ. His authority is our power, and His presence is everything to us. His presence is our regulation, His presence is our creed, His presence is our teaching and our preaching. As long as we have His presence, we need nothing more and we want nothing more. Praise the Lord we have it. Hallelujah!

CHAPTER SEVEN

CHRIST, THE LIFE-IMPARTING ONE

Scripture Reading: John 5:1-18, 21, 24-26, 39-40, 46-47; 6:63

We have been in the first book of the four Gospels, Matthew, and now we come to the last, John. The record of all four Gospels from the beginning to the end shows how Christ is versus religion and religion is always against Christ. According to the dictionary, religion is not a bad word; in a sense it is good. To be religious is much better than being sinful, fleshly, or worldly. But in the passage we have read in John 5:1-18 we see how dreadful religion really is. In this passage we see a group of religious people who pay attention to their sabbath and their God. They are violently opposed to Jesus. They have two main things against Him: 1) He broke the sabbath, and 2) He made Himself equal to God, to their God. They not only opposed Him, but even attempted to kill Him. Have you ever realized that this is the attitude of religion toward Jesus? These were not sinful people; neither were they what we think of as worldly people; they were religious, and they were for God. Yet they did whatever they could to annihilate Jesus. Jesus is the target of all the arrows of religion. We must see this.

The situation is the very same today. The more we live by Jesus, the more we minister Christ to people, the more the religious people will hate us. But be clear, we are versus them, but we do not hate them. The religious people hated Jesus, but Jesus never hated them. Jesus was one hundred percent versus religion, but He still loved those religious people.

We have seen three main points in the Gospel of

Matthew: firstly, that Jesus is our Bridegroom for our present enjoyment; secondly, that Jesus is the way whereby we may find rest; and thirdly, that Jesus is our Lawgiver and Prophet, He is today's Moses and our present Elijah. Let me say again that I do like Matthew. Matthew in the first chapter tells us that Jesus is Emmanuel, God with us. Then after giving us such a wonderful presentation of Jesus as our Bridegroom, our rest, our Lawgiver, and our Prophet, he says in the last chapter that this Jesus is with us "all the days, until the completion of the age" (v. 20 Gk.). Hallelujah, we have such a Jesus! We have this Emmanuel as so many items to us today. We may well be crazy for Christ since He is so much to us. But we not only have Matthew; we still have John.

THE THIRD SABBATH

The situation in John regarding Christ and religion is nearly the same as that in Matthew. We will skip over the first four chapters and come immediately to the fifth chapter. Here, you see, it was another sabbath day (v. 9). I will call this the third sabbath day. On the first sabbath, Christ took care of Himself as the Head; on the second sabbath, He took care of the withered members of His Body. Now we come to the third sabbath. Later, we will see yet another sabbath. There were sabbath days after sabbath days. The Lord Jesus undoubtedly did something deliberately to break the sabbath day. Here, on the third sabbath, He came to a certain pool in Jerusalem. There are seven days in a week—why did Jesus not come to this pool on some other day? He did it purposely; He did it to break the religious regulations. The keeping of the sabbath is the first and greatest regulation of the Jewish religion. To the Jews, nothing beside God Himself is more important than keeping the sabbath. Jesus said in effect, "You Jews regard the sabbath so highly, but I, Jesus, am purposely doing something to break it." The Lord Jesus is a real "troublemaker."

Many times you have something of which you wish Jesus would keep His hands off—but He comes today, and He comes tomorrow, and He comes the following day to interfere. You know the story. The Lord Jesus knows how to make "trouble" for us. It is better to learn never to say no to Him. If we say no, He will come the next day, and then the third day, and then the fourth day. He will come again and again to drive the point home. To the Jews, He came on the sabbath again and again and again.

If you were a Jew, you surely would have been angry. You would have said, "Didn't we tell you that it's unlawful to heal on the sabbath? Yet you come again. What's the matter with you?" Jesus was out to make "trouble" for religion. He was saying, "You keep religion, but I break religion."

This particular sabbath day, as recorded in John 5, was probably not a common one. It may have been at a feast of the Jews. Here in this passage, in addition to the feast, are recorded the best things of the Jewish religion: of course, there is the holy city, Jerusalem; then we have a pool with five porches; next we have the water, which an angel from heaven occasionally stirred; lastly, we have the sabbath. There was the feast to make people happy and the sabbath to give them rest. But do you think that all those impotent ones at the pool could be happy or restful? Here is the best religion with all the best things of that religion. But if you would partake of the goodness of this religion, you must be so strong that you could be number one. If you could get into the pool first, then you could share the benefit of that religion.

There was one among those impotent folk who was lying there for thirty-eight years, just the length of time the people of Israel wandered in the wilderness. The religion was good, the holy city was marvelous, the pool was wonderful, and the water was so inviting, with the very angels of heaven stirring it up—but what good is it all if I have no strength? The sick man complained, "Sir, I have no man, when the water is troubled, to put me into the pool..." (v. 7). In religion there is no help. Why? Because everybody hardly has enough to help himself; no one has anything to spare for others. Religion was good, but it was not good for him. It was good, but he could not partake of it. He was impotent, he was powerless, he was weak. This was the situation.

"ARISE, TAKE UP THY BED, AND WALK"

But listen, suddenly a man came—not a big man, but the little Jesus. Nobody paid any attention to Him. He had no form, no comeliness; He was one who came from Galilee, from that little town of Nazareth. Jesus came and saw the impotent man lying there. This is marvelous! We did not come to Jesus; He came to us. And when He came, we paid no attention to Him; yet He looked upon us. "When Jesus saw him lying, and knew that he had been now a long time in that case, He saith unto him, wouldst thou be made whole?" (v. 6). Now listen to the foolish religious talk: "Sir, I have no man, when the water is troubled, to put me into the pool: but while I am coming, another steppeth down before me." While he was speaking nonsense, the Lord Jesus commanded, "Arise, take up thy bed, and walk." What does this mean? This simply means, "Forget about that religious nonsense. I'm not interested." I tell you, this is Jesus. He told him not only to rise, but to take up his bed. The bed carried him for thirty-eight years; now Jesus told him to carry it. What would you do? Would you still say, "O Lord, I am still so impotent, and when the water moves no one will come to help me"? Many times, we simply like to talk religious nonsense. Would we be willing to forget it all? The Lord Jesus said, "Do not talk any more, but rise, take up your bed and walk." If we will drop our religion and take Jesus' living word, we will be healed and receive life. That day the impotent man was healed, and that day was the sabbath.

THE RELIGIOUS PEOPLE INFURIATED

Then the Jews saw what was done to the impotent man and came to him saying, "What! Are you taking up your bed and walking on the sabbath day? Don't you know it's not lawful to do this. It is lawful to lie there impotent, but it is not lawful to get up and walk. It is lawful for you to be dead, but it is not lawful for you to be alive." I tell you, this is today's Christianity.

So many people today criticize us for shouting and noisily praising the Lord. What about so many dead ones in the denominations? Why don't they criticize them? Why don't they condemn that? They are just like the Jews. They would rather keep their religious regulations than see someone made alive.

The man who was made whole answered them, "He that made me whole, the same said unto me, take up thy bed, and walk" (v. 11). He said in other words, "If this is wrong, it is not my mistake; it is His mistake. The One who made me whole told me to rise, take up my bed and walk." They said then, "All right, you are not to be blamed. Who is that man who told you to do this?" He replied, "I do not know." Then, later, Jesus met the man, and the man went to tell the Jews that it was Jesus. Oh! The Jews were so furious that they set about to kill Him.

Jesus spoke then to the Jews, "My Father worketh even until now, and I work" (v. 17). He said in other words, "You are keeping the sabbath, but My Father is working all the time, and I am working with Him. I work because My Father's work has not yet been accomplished." This infuriated them even more. Now this little Jesus was not only breaking the Sabbath, but making Himself equal with God. They were intent upon getting rid of Him.

NOT RELIGION, BUT LIFE

Then Jesus went on to say, "As the Father raiseth the dead and giveth them life, even so the Son also giveth life to whom He will" (v. 21). What is this? This is Christ

versus religion. We must all realize today it is not a
matter of religion, but of Christ as the very God
imparting life to us. This is all we need. We need a Christ
who is equal to God and who is God Himself, imparting
life to us. And the way He imparts life to us is not by
any religion, forms, doctrines, teachings, or regulations,
but by His living Word. "Verily, verily, I say unto you, He
that heareth my Word, and believeth Him that sent Me.
hath eternal life, and cometh not into judgment, but hath
passed out of death into life" (v. 24). Whoever hears His
living Word and receives it has eternal life. This is all—it
is so simple.

NOT THE SCRIPTURES. BUT CHRIST

Then the Lord Jesus turned again to the Jews and
said, "Ye search the scriptures..." (v. 39). The English
translation of the word "search" is not adequate. In the
Greek it means "research." The Lord Jesus was saying,
"Ye search and research the scriptures, because ye think
that in them ye have eternal life." This was their
imagination: they thought that they could find life in the
Scriptures. But the Lord Jesus said to them, "Beside Me,
without Me. regardless of how many times you read the
Scriptures, you cannot have life." To say that in the Bible
there is life is in a sense a kind of imagination. Life.
strictly speaking, is not in the Scriptures, but in Christ.
If you have Christ with the Scriptures, surely you will
have life; but if you have the Scriptures. but are devoid
of the living Christ as the life-giving Spirit, you have no
life. If you say you do, that is a game, that is your
imagination. "Ye search the scriptures" Jesus said "because ye think that in them ye have life but really you
do not. What you have is just deadness. The more you
search, the more dead you are. The letter kills. Ye search
the Scriptures. but ye will not come to Me that ye may
have life."

Brothers and sisters, never forget verses 39 and 40 of
John 5. It is these two verses in the entire Bible which

show us that to search the Scripture is one thing, and
to come to the Lord for life is another. It is entirely
possible to search and even research the Scriptures, yet
never to touch the living Christ as the life-giving Spirit.
When I was young I did much searching and re-
searching of the Bible. But, Hallelujah, today I have given
it up. Today I just come to the living Christ through the
living word of the Bible. Whenever I open the Scriptures,
I firstly touch the Lord. I open my mouth and say, "O
Lord Jesus, I come to You." Brothers, never come to this
living Book without coming to the living Lord Jesus. If
you do, you will simply be religious.

Why do you read the Scriptures? Because there is life
in the Scriptures? It is indeed a wonderful and marvelous
Book. But look at those who spend so much time in Bible
study. Do not misunderstand me: I respect the Bible, and
I have spent very much time in its pages. But I have
found one thing: we should never read the Bible without
touching the living Christ. If you separate the Bible from
Christ, then Christ is versus your Bible. Christianity
today almost makes the Scriptures a book of dead letters.
So Christ in this sense versus the Scriptures. People take
this Book for knowledge and even obtain degrees in Bible
study, but they utterly miss Christ. He said, "Ye search
the scriptures...and ye will not come to Me, that ye may
have life."

You may say that the Bible testifies of Christ. Undoubtedly. Even Moses spoke of Christ in all his writings.
But you should not separate all those writings from the
living, present Christ. You need to wed all the Scriptures
to Christ; then you will have the life; then you will have
the living Word. The Lord said, "It is the Spirit that
giveth life...the words that I have spoken unto you are
spirit, and are life" (John 6:63). The words, the Lord said,
are spirit; so they must be taken as the Spirit and in
the Spirit. It is the Spirit that gives life; the letter kills
(2 Cor. 3:6). If you take the Bible just as letters, you
receive death, not life. All the words in the Bible proceeded

out of the mouth of the very Lord who is the Spirit; so whatever comes from Him must also be Spirit, for He Himself is the Spirit. Every word of the Bible must be taken as the Spirit that gives life. If we exercise our mind to research the Scriptures, we make every word of the Bible dead letters. If, however, we exercise our spirit to contact the Word by calling on His name, it is life. There is no other way to make this word, printed in black and white, so living, as the Spirit to us. We must read it by calling on the name of the Lord Jesus from deep within. Mingle your reading and calling on the Lord as one. Then you will get the life.

TWO KEYS—THE SPIRIT AND THE WORD

We have seen firstly that Christ is our happiness, secondly that He is our rest, thirdly that He is our Lawgiver and Predictor, and fourthly that He is the One who imparts life to us. How rich are all these items! Yet how may we touch such a Christ? What are the keys to open the doors? He has said, "Lo, I am with you all the days until the completion of the age"; but how can we enjoy Him? How can we contact Him? Two things are the keys—the Spirit and the Word.

The most precious verse in John chapter 3 is verse 6: "That which is born of the Spirit is spirit." Then in John 4, the most precious verse is verse 24: "God is Spirit: and they that worship Him must worship in spirit and truth." In these two chapters of John, two spirits are mentioned: one with a capital letter 'S' and the other with a small letter 's.' We know that the one with the capital letter is the Holy Spirit, and the one with the small letter refers to our human spirit. Christ is so much, and Christ is everything to us; but whatever Christ is, is altogether the Spirit. He is the life-giving Spirit. This wonderful Christ who is today the Spirit is in our spirit, and the two spirits, the divine and the human, have been mingled together as one. "That which is born of the Spirit is spirit." "God is Spirit: and they that worship Him must worship in spirit."

But when we pass through chapters 3 and 4 of John and come to chapters 5 and 6, something more is added. Here in chapter 5, we read, "He that heareth my Word" (v. 24), and "The dead shall hear the voice of the Son of God" (v. 25). So we not only have the Spirit, but also the Word.

THE WORD IS THE SPIRIT, AND THE SPIRIT IS THE WORD

In chapter 5 we have not only the living Word, but also the written Word. Jesus said to the Jewish people, "Ye research the scriptures"—the written Word. He said also, "For if ye believed Moses, ye would believe Me; for he wrote of Me. But if ye believe not his writings, how shall ye believe my words?" (vv. 46-47). Again Jesus referred to the written Word. He told them that if they did not believe the written Word of the Bible, how could they believe the living Word out of His mouth? So today, praise the Lord, we have the written Word. We have the Spirit, and we have the Word. Then, when we come to chapter 6, verse 63, the Lord Jesus makes these two things one. He said, "It is the Spirit that gives life...the words that I have spoken unto you are spirit." Firstly we are told that it is by the Spirit that we touch Christ, and then we see that it also through the Word that we contact Him. Eventually, the Lord Jesus reveals to us that these two are one: the Word is the Spirit, and the Spirit is the Word.

John 6: 63 is a verse which strongly proves that the Word is the Spirit. There is another verse in the Bible, however, which tells us that the Spirit is the Word. Let me give you the literal translation, word for word, from the Greek text of Ephesians 6:17-18. "And take ye the helmet of salvation, and the sword of the Spirit, which Spirit is the Word of God, by means of all prayer and petition, praying at every time in spirit..." Here in these two verses of Scripture, three main points are revealed: 1) The Spirit is the Word. Have you ever realized that the Spirit of God is the Word? Not only is the Word the

Spirit, but also the Spirit is the Word. 2) By what means may we take this Word? We are told here to take the Word of God "by means of all prayer and petition." This is pray-reading. We must not take the Word of God by merely reading, but by prayer, and by all prayer. There are all kinds of prayer. Sometimes we need to take the Word by praying quietly; at other times we must take the Word by praying aloud; and there are times when we must also take the Word by shouting to the Lord. Sometimes we need to take the Word by short prayers; at other times we must take it by long prayers. Sometimes we need to pray-read individually; at other times we need to pray the Word together with a few others; and sometimes we must pray-read with a large congregation. There are many ways. But the principle is one—we must take the Word of God "by means of all prayer and petition." 3) These verses also tell us how we must pray—"praying at every time in spirit [our human spirit]." We must exercise our spirit, the deepest part of our being, to pray the Word. Do not analyze the Word, do not research the Word; just take it by praying in the spirit. Hallelujah! What are the two keys whereby we may contact Christ? The Holy Spirit and the Holy Word. We have the Holy Spirit in our spirit, and we have the Holy Word, the Bible, in our hands. These should not be two things, but two ends of one thing. The end within us is the Spirit; the end outside of us is the Word. When the Word enters our spirit it becomes the Spirit, and when the Spirit is expressed from our mouth it becomes the Word. You see, the Spirit and the Word, the Word and the Spirit, are two ends of one thing. The inner end is the Spirit, and the outer end is the Word. When the outer end gets into our spirit it becomes the Spirit, and when the inner end proceeds from our mouth, it becomes the Word. These are the two keys for us to contact Christ. Christ today is the Spirit and is in the Word. Forget about religion. Forget about doctrine, teaching, forms, rituals,

rules and regulations. Just take care of Christ. Contact
Christ as the Spirit and in the Word.

THE ORGAN TO USE THE KEYS

What is the organ for us to use these two keys? It is
our human spirit. Our hand, we know, is the proper organ
to turn the key to open the door of our house. To somehow
manipulate our mouth or our toes to turn the key would
be extremely absurd. Likewise, the proper organ for us
to use the keys of the Spirit and the Word is not our
mentality or our will, but our human spirit. We must
exercise our human spirit; we must stay in the spirit.
Whenever we pray, we must pray in our spirit; whenever
we pray-read the Word, we must pray-read with our spirit;
whenever we say, "O Lord, Amen, Hallelujah," we must
say it by exercising our human spirit. The Bible may
either be a book of letters or a book full of words as the
Spirit. The kind of Bible we have depends upon which
organ we use to contact it. If we contact the Bible by our
mentality, it is merely a book of letters to us. If we
contact the Bible, however, by exercising our spirit, it
immediately becomes a book of the Spirit. The Apostle
Paul said in 2 Corinthians 3:6, "The letter killeth, but
the Spirit giveth life." Paul, in referring to the letter
which kills, was referring to the written Scriptures. If
we contact the Scriptures with our mind, it becomes the
killing letters. The same book may be either killing letters
or the life-giving Spirit.

We all must realize firstly that we have such a
Christ—a Christ for our happiness, a Christ for our rest,
a Christ as our Lawgiver and Predictor, and a Christ as
the Life-giver. But we must also realize that this Christ
today is the Spirit and is in the Word. Now, if we would
contact this Christ, we need to exercise our spirit to
pray-read the Word or simply to call on His name. If we
would do this, we would continually contact Christ and
enjoy Him. There is no other way.

Have you ever changed your way in dealing with the

Bible? I am much concerned that you are still cleaving to your old way of reading and studying the Bible by exercising your mentality. Are you still in the old way? Sometimes, no doubt, in your study of the Bible you have received some life. But I believe that most of the time you have been deadened and killed. It is simply because you have used the wrong way. The new way and best way is that whenever you come to the Bible, at the same time you come to the Lord. Always combine coming to the Bible with coming to the Lord. When you come to the Bible, you must open your spirit and mouth to call on the name of the Lord Jesus. Whatever verse, whatever sentence you read, read it by calling on the name of the Lord. Always mingle your reading of the Scriptures with calling on the Lord Jesus. Try it! You will see the difference.

You may say then, "Should we not understand the Bible?" Leave this matter to the Lord. Just pray-read; the Lord will take care of your understanding. I guarantee that if you faithfully pray-read the Word of God, you will understand the Bible much better than all the others who do not pray-read.

Let us use for an illustration a match. The match stick, it is true, is made of wood, but in essence the match is really phosphorus. The meaning of the word phosphorus is "light-bearer." II Peter 1:19 refers to the Lord as the day-star: that term "day-star" in Greek is the word phosphorus. Christ is the phosphorus, the light-bearer, shining in the darkness. Now suppose I want to use the match: what shall I do? Of course, I must strike it. But how shall I strike it? If I strike it, using the end without the phosphorus, though I strike till eternity I will get no light. I am using the wrong end. The Bible is the match, and the Lord Jesus, the Spirit, is the phosphorus. The wooden stick may be likened to the black and white letters, the words in the Bible, which hold Christ as the phosphorus, the heavenly day-star. How can we make the phosphorus take fire and shine? We must use the right end of the match, and we must strike it on the right spot.

The right end is the Holy Spirit, and the right spot is our human spirit. We must not care so much for the black and white letters—that is tantamount to concentrating on the wooden stick of the match. All our focus should be on the end with the phosphorus. We do have the letters of the written Word, but we must not pay too much attention to them. We must concentrate on the heavenly phosphorus in the Word, Christ the Spirit. And we must strike this end in the right place, our human spirit. How many Christians there are who are "striking" the Bible in the area of their mentality. Little wonder that they never catch fire. We need the stick to hold the phosphorus, no doubt; we need the written Word, the black and white letters, to contain Christ, the heavenly phosphorus. But it is the phosphorus, it is the Spirit, that burns and gives the light. We must strike the right end, and we must strike the right end at the right spot. We must take the written Word and strike the Lord who is the Spirit upon our human spirit. Immediately we will get the fire. It really works. If you stay with the Bible for half an hour or even an hour and get no fire, you are wrong. I can tell you, just after two minutes of, "O Lord Jesus! In the beginning was the Word. Amen! O Lord Jesus, You are the Word! Amen, Lord Jesus! Hallelujah!" you will be burned. This is the right way to contact the Word. You have to strike the Lord Jesus, the heavenly phosphorus in the Word, upon your human spirit. Hallelujah! Try the new way, and you will give up the old way. Every time you come to the Word in this new way it will burn and shine upon you.

Praise the Lord, we have the keys, we have the organ, and we have the way to contact and enjoy such a wonderful Christ.

CHAPTER EIGHT

CHRIST GIVING SIGHT

Scripture Reading: John 9:1-3, 6-7, 14-16, 22, 24-25, 28-30, 33-38; 10:1-11, 14-16, 21, 26-31, 38-39

Now we come to chapter 9 of John, where we find another sabbath. We have already passed through three sabbaths, and now we come to the fourth. In all of them the Lord Jesus did something to break them. The Lord Jesus always acted deliberately and intentionally to break the sabbath. He was an excellent sabbath breaker. We must not think that it was just by accident that He performed these things on the sabbath day. No, He did it with a definite purpose. He did it to purposely break the regulations of religion.

A SABBATH REVIEW

Let us review briefly the sabbaths through which we have already passed. It is interesting that in the record of Matthew there are two sabbaths, and in the record of John there are another two sabbaths. The first sabbath was a case of hungry people: the Lord Jesus brought His disciples into the cornfield and gave them full freedom to do as they liked. The cornfield was not the synagogue or the temple; it was a rather wild and uncultured place. Would you rather sit in good order in a cultured synagogue, or would you prefer to be in the cornfield, plucking the ears of corn, without keeping any regulations? What kind of person would you prefer to be? The cornfield was an eating place, a place of liberty from all religious regulations.

The second sabbath was a case of a withered member, which the Lord Jesus likened to a sheep fallen into a pit. The withered member was the fallen sheep without rest. So the Lord broke the sabbath that the withered and fallen member might find rest. In the second case the object of the Lord's concern was not in the cornfield, but in the pit. When we are withered, we are simply in the pit; we are bound and have no rest. But, hallelujah, the Lord Jesus has lifted us up! The Lord Jesus has healed us, and now we are out of the pit and dwelling at home. The church is firstly a cornfield and then a home.

The third sabbath is the case of an impotent man lying in a religious porch, waiting for something to happen. The Lord Jesus saw him and by His word imparted life into him. The Lord Jesus has not only fed us and lifted us up, but imparted His life into us. Now we not only have satisfaction and freedom, but we are made alive.

A BLIND MAN IN THE FOLD

Now we come to the last sabbath, the fourth case. It is a case of a blind man. We may be whole and perfect in every sense and yet, like this man, be born blind. The only problem with this man was that he did not have sight. And the Lord Jesus clearly implies in the following chapter of John, chapter 10, that this very man was one who was in the "fold." In one sense the fold is a good place, but in another sense the fold is not good. The fold, you know, is the place where the flock is kept at night, in the wintertime, or when a storm is raging. In the day, when the sun is shining, the sheep should not be in the fold, but on the pasture. The destiny of a blind man, however, is to be in the fold, kept and preserved in the night. A blind man never has a sunny day: even if the sun is shining, he cannot enjoy it. To the blind man, the day is as the night; he is always in darkness. If you are blind, you are in the fold.

When we were in the denominations, we were blind. I do not believe that any dear Christians who have really received sight from the Lord could still remain in the denominations. Everyone who sees must leave the fold and enter the pasture, under the sunshine, in the fresh air, in liberty. Where are you now? Are you in the fold, or are you now in the pasture? Allow me to say this: if anyone is still in the fold, he is blind. Of course, a blind person requires the fold to keep him. But when he receives his sight, he will swiftly leave the fold for the pasture, for the sunshine, for the fresh air.

A PICTURE OF OUR CONDITION

Do not think that these four cases on these four sabbaths are speaking of four different persons. I tell you, spiritually speaking, these four cases are four aspects of one person—us. We are the hungry ones, we are the withered members and fallen sheep, we are those who have been impotent for so many years, and we are just as the blind man. We are hungry, withered, fallen, impotent and blind. Before we were saved, before we were brought into the church life, we were this kind of person. This is a real portrait of our condition at that time. I can testify that before I was saved and came into the church life I was really hungry, I was so withered and fallen, so impotent and blind. In one sense I was waiting for something to happen, and in another sense I was truly blind. I did not know in what direction I was moving; I could not discern whether it was day or night. I was in the fold. But, hallelujah, the Lord Jesus came to feed us by breaking the sabbath. Hallelujah, the Lord Jesus came also to lift us up out of the pit by breaking the regulations of religion. And the Lord Jesus came to impart life into us. Formerly, we relied on something happening to us, but now we can take up our bed and walk; we have life. And the Lord Jesus did this also by again breaking the regulations of religion. Eventually, hallelujah, the Lord Jesus came and opened our eyes, and we were cast out of the fold by the religious people into the pasture.

Hallelujah! How wonderful to be cast out of the fold into the pasture!

Now in the church life we are no longer hungry—we are in the cornfield. Now in the church life we are no longer in the pit—we are at home. Now in the church life we are no longer lying impotent in a religious porch—we have life; there is no need for others to help us, now we can carry everything. Now in the church life we are no longer in the fold—we are on the pasture. It is joy unspeakable and full of glory!

Eventually we are not only on the pasture, but also in the flock—praise the Lord! We are not a fold but a flock. The fold is a place to keep us, but the flock is a composition of all the saints. The church is not a place; the church is a flock. If we are a denomination, if we are a synagogue, if we are a sect, then surely we are a fold. But, hallelujah, we have all been flocked together as the church. We are the flocked sheep on the green and tender pasture, enjoying the unlimited Christ all the time. Are there any regulations? No. Are there any forms? No. Is there any bondage? No. We have green pasture, we have liberty, we have life, we have open air, we have sunshine, we have all we need. We have one flock with one Shepherd. This is where we are today. Are you there? The Lord broke all these four sabbaths to bring us here.

NEITHER YES NOR NO

Let us now consider the case of the blind man in more detail. The Lord Jesus passing by saw this man blind from his birth. And His disciples asked Him, "Rabbi, who sinned, this man, or his parents, that he should be born blind?" (9:2). The disciples' question was entirely religious. Since the man was blind, they reasoned, someone must have sinned, either he or his parents. But Jesus answered, "Neither did this man sin, nor his parents" (v. 3). If you read the Gospel of John carefully, you will see that people frequently came to Jesus with questions requiring a yes or no answer. But Jesus never answered yes or no. He always said in effect, "Neither yes, nor no." For example, the Samaritan woman in chapter 4 introduced the matter of worship. She said, "Our fathers worshipped in this mountain: and ye say, that in Jerusalem is the place where men ought to worship" (v. 20). But the Lord Jesus replied, "Neither in this mountain, nor in Jerusalem, shall ye worship the Father" (v. 21). The Lord's answer to His disciples in chapter 9 was of a similar nature. The Lord Jesus never answers yes or no; He always answers according to life. With Him, it is not a matter of right or wrong, yes or no, good or evil, or anything of the tree of knowledge; it is entirely a matter of God, a matter of life. The Lord Jesus told His disciples, "Neither did this man sin, nor his parents: but that the works of God should be made manifest in him" (v. 3). The question of the disciples was one of religion; the answer of the Lord Jesus was one of revelation. Jesus took away the veil of religion: He said in effect, "Forget about religion. It is not a matter of this or that, but a matter of the work of God being manifested."

DIVINITY MINGLES WITH HUMANITY

The Lord Jesus spoke very little after this. Immediately following this statement of His we read that He spat on the ground and made clay of the spittle (v. 6). Scientifically and culturally speaking, spittle is a very dirty substance. But the Lord Jesus spat on the ground and even mixed the spittle with the clay. Then, with this spittle, we read, the Lord anointed the eyes of the blind man and told him to go and wash. He did, and he returned healed. The Lord Jesus in performing this sign acted not in a miraculous way, but in an uncultured, unrefined way, totally contrary to human concept. People would say that what He did was coarse and foolish. Who would ever think that the Lord Jesus would use spittle mingled with dirt, of all things, as a kind of ointment to anoint a blind man. But the Lord is always acting contrary to our religious and human concept. Spiritually speaking, what He did is full of meaning. Something out of the mouth of the Lord was mingled with something of the ground. We are the ground. Therefore, what the Lord did signifies the mingling of divinity with humanity.

We were all born blind. In what way did we receive sight? By being mingled with the Lord Jesus as a divine Person. Some element of Christ must enter into us and be come mingled with us. Most of us can testify from our experience: the day we received Christ was the day we received our sight. Even today, there is no other way to receive sight, but by the mingling of Christ within us. Let Christ put something of Himself into you, and you will receive sight.

NEITHER RIGHT NOR WRONG

The man received sight. It was wonderful. Again the Pharisees, the religionists, were on hand to condemn. They discouraged this poor man who received his sight from following Jesus. Reviling him, they said, "Thou art His disciple; but we are disciples of Moses" (v. 28). They called Jesus a sinner because He broke the sabbath, but the blind man exclaimed, "Whether He is a sinner, I know not: one thing I know, that, whereas I was blind, now I see" (v. 25). The blind man didn't care about right or wrong; he only cared that he received his sight. Whether right or wrong, whether yes or no—it mattered nothing to him. He only cared for seeing.

CAST OUT OF RELIGION

They reviled him. In that day to say that you were a follower of Jesus was a vile thing. Then they cast him out. They cast him out of the synagogue, out of Judaism, out of the Jewish religion. Hallelujah! But we must realize that in that day to be cast out of the Jewish synagogue and religion meant that there was no way to live. You could not keep your job; your living was ended. To be an outcast from the Jewish religion in that day was very serious. But the Lord Jesus met him and asked, "Dost thou believe on the Son of God?" (v. 35). He answered and said, "And who is He, Lord, that I may believe on Him?"

Jesus replied, "Thou hast both seen Him, and He it is that speaketh with thee." And he said, "Lord, I believe," and he worshipped Him. Today, when we read the record, we feel that it was so simple and not of too much consequence; but, I tell you, in that day it was not so simple, and it was of tremendous consequence.

CHRIST, THE DOOR OF THE FOLD

Immediately upon the casting out of this man from the synagogue the Lord Jesus gave the people a message, telling how He is the door of all the sheep within the sheepfold. He said that all who came before Him were thieves and robbers; He is the only one who came to impart life to the sheep. He is the One who leads the sheep out of the fold, through the door, into the pasture— He is the Shepherd. He also told them that He had other sheep which were not of that Jewish fold—them also would He bring, and they would be flocked together with the sheep from the sheepfold to be one flock. It is all so meaningful.

Many dear saints, when reading that Jesus is the door in John chapter 10, conceive of Jesus as the door to heaven. That concept is utterly mistaken. In John chapter 10, Jesus is the door, not of heaven, but of the fold. Judaism, the Jewish religion, was the fold. We must realize that this fold was firstly established by God in the Old Testament. God put all His dear saints into it to be kept, waiting for Christ to come. They were put there, not over the walls, but through the door, and that door was Christ. David was put there, Jeremiah was put there, Daniel was put there. They were all put into the fold through the proper gate, Christ. Those Old Testament saints who believed in the coming Christ found entrance to the fold through Him. Christ was the door through which they entered. Then Jesus came; the night was over and the day had dawned. There was no need for the sheep to be kept in the fold any longer; they must go out and find pasture. The winter was over, spring had come; Christ, the pasture, was there. Before He came, Jesus was the door by which they all came in. Then when he came, He said in effect, "Now I am the door for you all to get out." In the Old Testament time Christ was the door for the saints to enter the fold, and now in the New Testament time He is the door for all the sheep who are in the fold to come out. Then when he leads them out, He's not only the door, but also the Shepherd. They are the sheep, and He is the Shepherd, leading them to the green pasture. And He is the pasture too. He led Peter out of the fold, He led John out of the fold, He led James out of the fold, and He led this blind one who received sight out of the fold.

Then He told the people that He had other sheep in the Gentile world, the heathen world. Later He came to America, a part of the heathen world. One day, praise the Lord, the Lord Jesus also came to my country, another part of the heathen world. We are all the other sheep, and He brought us all together on His green pasture. We are one flock.

When Jesus walked on earth, Judaism was the fold, but today there are new folds. There are so many denominations, sects, and Christian groups—all these in the eyes of the Lord are today's folds. Although people within these groups may have good intentions as far as the Lord is concerned, yet the result is disastrous—the result is division. They may intend to keep the people of the Lord as a fold, but eventually they cause a division. The Lord today is doing the same work as He did in John chapter 9: He is opening the eyes of many who are held by the folds; He is leading them out of the folds and putting them together on the green pasture as one flock. After you receive your sight, those who run the folds will no longer be willing to keep you there, and on the other hand you will be quite willing to come out. Christ is the door for you to come out and join the one flock with the one Shepherd.

FROM RELIGION TO THE CHURCH

Originally we were hungry, fallen, impotent, and blind.

Hallelujah, today we are the flock, the church, the Bride for the Bridegroom. Today we are no more in the pit, no more in the religious porches, no more in the fold, but on the pasture which is Christ Himself. We have been lifted out of the pit, released from the porch, led out of the fold, and flocked together as the one flock with one Shepherd, feeding on the green pasture. This is the church life.

Let us return now briefly to see how the trouble between the Lord Jesus and religion began. According to the record of the four Gospels, it all started with the matter of fasting and praying. The Lord Jesus came into an atmosphere utterly impregnated with religion, and the break began. It did not start with Him or from Him, but from the religious people, the disciples of John and of the Pharisees. We have already seen how they came to the Lord Jesus inquiring about fasting. That was the beginning of the break. The Lord did not keep fasting; He broke this religious thing. Following His breaking of the fasting system, He began to break the sabbath—the four cases we have seen. When we come to the last case, we have come to the climax. This is the ultimate station; we do not need the fifth sabbath. Now we are on the mountain top; now we have a flock, and we are the flock, the church. We reach this point by coming out of the fold through the door, by following Him under His shepherding, and by enjoying Him day by day in all His riches as our pasture. It is by this that we are all together. We are not organized together; we are flocked together by the Lord Jesus as the door, the Shepherd, and the pasture. It is by this that we become the church, the ultimate, eternal intention of God. Everything is now accomplished. It is all His wonderful doing.

It was in 1932 that I first came into the local church. The Lord Jesus led me out of the "synagogue" into the "cornfield" to feed on its riches. Oh, the church to me at that time was just like the cornfield: I could pick all the ears and enjoy the corn. Then He lifted me up out of the pit; I was a withered member, I was waiting in the porch, waiting for something or someone, but He imparted life into me and made me an active member of the Body. I was impotent, I was blind, but He put something of Himself into me, not just that I might have life, but that I might have it abundantly, and in so doing I received my sight. Then I was made clear; I could see Him as the door and follow Him out of the fold into the pasture. Now I can testify that day and night I am on the pasture enjoying Him. How good it is to be in the flock! Hallelujah, we are flocked together. We never try to unite; we are flocked together. We are not united by any charters or creeds made by human hands; we are united by the Lord Jesus as the door, the Shepherd, and the pasture.

When the flock comes into being, everything is completed. Now we really have a Sabbath. We do not break this Sabbath; we keep this Sabbath for eternity. Day by day we are resting in Christ, we are enjoying the real Sabbath. All the working sabbaths are over; we are now in the resting Sabbath. We are resting in the flock.

JOHN TEN INTERPRETS JOHN NINE

Chapter 10 of the Gospel of John must be put together with chapter 9: these are not two separate records, but one record in two chapters. In chapter 10 the Lord Jesus said, "The thief cometh not, but that he may steal, and kill, and destroy: I came that they may have life, and may have it abundantly" (v. 10). Many times we have quoted this verse in an isolated way, neglecting the context. Now, by putting these two chapters together, we see the way whereby the Lord imparts life to us. The blind man was there, a man made of mere clay. But the Lord Jesus healed him and recovered his sight by emitting something out of His mouth and mingling it with the clay. With such a strange kind of ointment, the man was anointed and healed. Without chapter 10, it is rather difficult to understand the significance of the Lord's act in mingling the spittle with the clay. Chapter 10 interprets it by showing that in so doing He imparted life: something out from Him entered into the blind man and mingled with him. What the Lord did in chapter 9 was a sign, signifying a spiritual reality. The Lord Jesus came to impart life to us by something coming out of His mouth and mingling with us. When we come to chapter 20 of this Gospel, we see how the Lord Jesus after His resurrection came to His disciples and breathed into them. This breathing was in a sense a kind of spitting. Something came out of His mouth and entered into His disciples, mingling with them as with the clay. That is the imparting of life. Life is nothing else but something of the Lord Jesus breathed into us and mingled with us. It is by the life then that we receive the sight.

THE WAY TO PRACTICE
THE MINGLING

In what way could we have something coming out from the Lord and into us to mingle with us today? In either of two ways: 1) By calling upon His name. When we call upon His name, we breathe Him in. 2) By pray-reading His Word. The spittle today is the living Word, and we are the pieces of clay. The more we pray-read, the more something of the Lord Jesus comes out from Him and into us. It is thus that something of the Lord is mingled with us, and we not only have life, but have it abundantly. It is by this life, then, that we are enabled to see.

You may say that whenever I speak I always return eventually to the matter of calling on the name of the Lord and pray-reading. It is really so. I have not found a third way. In all my years of experience with the Lord, I have only found these two ways: calling on the name of the Lord and pray-reading the Word. I do know of a certainty that this is the best way for the Lord to mingle something of Himself with us.

Do you realize that you are merely a piece of clay, born blind and kept in a fold? If so, you must let Christ emit something out of Himself and into you. Then you will have life and receive the sight to see; you will be out of the fold and enjoy the pasture. There is no other way but by calling on His name and pray-reading. All the day we need to say, "O Lord, Amen! O Lord, Amen!" All the day we also need to pray-read the Word. Then the spittle from the mouth of the Lord will mingle with us the clay. We will have the anointing, for this is the anointing. Hallelujah! The more we call on the name of the Lord and pray-read the Word, the more we are anointed. This anointing is so sweet, so refreshing, so new. It is by this that we experience Christ as the door, the Shepherd, and the green pasture. And it is by this that we are now in the flock, the church.

Eventually we have nothing and keep nothing but Christ and the Church, the Head with the Body. The Lord in the last days of this age is recovering this; He is recovering Christ as life with the proper church life. Now the Lord is doing something to put the enemy to shame. God the Father can point to the enemy and say, "Satan, look, even on this earth, in this dark age, My Son Jesus Christ could have such a Body." Not only is this a shame to Satan, but also a beach head for Christ to gain the entire earth. The church life will be the beachhead for Christ to return. The Lord is doing this, not in a human way, but in a divine way; not in an organized way, but by the transforming Spirit.

Chapter Nine

THE LORD'S COMMISSION

Scripture Reading: John 20:1, 11, 14-17, 19-23, 26; 21:1, 3-6,
9-19, 22

Among the four Gospels there are two which indicate
how greatly Christ is versus religion—Matthew and John.
Why do Matthew and John record so much concerning
this matter? It is because Matthew declares that Jesus
is Emmanuel, God with us. He was not only a man, but
also God. As such He was absolutely other than religion;
as such He had nothing to do with religion. As a man
He might have religious associations and relationships,
but as God with us He is absolutely outside of religion.
This is Matthew. John then tells us that Jesus was the
Word in the beginning, God Himself, incarnated to be a
man. He was not just a man, but a God-man. Thus,
because of His essential being, He had nothing to do with
religion.

Another matter peculiar to Matthew and John is that
neither mentioned anything regarding the ascension of
the Lord Jesus. The Gospels of Mark and Luke, on the
other hand, both mention it. The ascension of the Lord
means that He has departed from us. But Matthew tells
us that He is Emmanuel, God with us. As such, He could
never depart. Therefore He said, "Lo, I am with you all
the days, even unto the completion of the age" (Matt.
28:20). The Bible tells us Jesus ascended, but Matthew
and John do not say so. There is no closing to the Gospel
of Matthew; neither is there a conclusion to the Gospel
of John. The record of John concerning the Lord Jesus
meeting on this earth with His disciples has not ended.

The Gospel of John in the heavens may already be of two thousand and twenty-two chapters. Now, perhaps, we are in the two thousand and twenty-third chapter. Such a Jesus certainly could not be in any religion. He must be outside of religion.

JOHN 21, AN APPENDIX

The Gospel of John, undoubtedly, is the most wonderful book in the Bible concerning life. When I was young, I appreciated the first chapter of this Gospel very much. It has a glorious start: "In the beginning was the Word, and the Word was with God, and the Word was God...in Him was life; and the life was the light of men." It is exceedingly high and profound. But when I came to the last chapter of John, chapter 21, I was amazed and confounded. That did not sound like a chapter of John. It says, "Peter saith unto them, I go a fishing. They say unto him, We also come with thee." Then they all went fishing, and through the whole night they caught nothing. Suddenly Jesus was there and spoke with them concerning the matter of eating, etc., etc. What kind of a chapter is this? John 14 about the Comforter and the Spirit of reality, John 15 concerning the vine and the branches, and John 17, the Lord's high priestly prayer, are all marvelous, wonderful, and profound. Could you believe that such a book as John would contain a chapter like chapter 21? When I was young I thought that something must be wrong. In my opinion this chapter simply did not fit.

Let us look at the last two verses of chapter 20, verses 30 and 31: "Many other signs therefore did Jesus in the presence of the disciples, which are not written in this book: but these are written that ye may believe that Jesus is the Christ, the Son of God; and that believing ye may have life in His name." These verses are truly wonderful. They are an appropriate conclusion to the book. We may say that at this point the book is really closed. But after this, there is still another chapter. We might call it an appendix, a "P.S."

NO SCHEDULE

If you were Jesus and realized that you were going to die and be raised from the dead, surely you would have made many arrangements with your disciples. You would have said, "Peter, John, James, and the rest of you, come here and let me give you a schedule. Firstly I am going to die; secondly, I will be raised from the dead on the third day; thirdly, you must all meet me at a certain place, where I will do certain things among you; fourthly, you must all go to other places, where certain other things will happen; fifthly, sixthly, etc., etc., to number twenty-four." If you were Jesus, you would probably outline it in detail to the disciples. This is our natural concept; this is our religious mind. But read the last two chapters of John—there is no such thing; the Lord Jesus never made any arrangements or left any schedule. From our natural viewpoint, what was done was a mess. Everything occurred as a kind of accident. But, praise the Lord, though they had no schedule, no arrangements, no appointments, they had the resurrected Christ, the living Lord Jesus. This Christ, according to the record of these two chapters, came to His disciples at any time and in any place. He just came! He came in a way which was absolutely different from today's religion. He never came to a formal meeting—there never was one. If Peter should call an urgent meeting and gather all the disciples to discuss their problems with Jesus, that would fit our concept. But Jesus never met with His disciples in that way.

JESUS APPEARS
TO FOOLISH SISTERS

Following Jesus' resurrection, His first appearance was to a group of foolish sisters. In a sense, the sisters in the church life are always the foolish ones. Mentally, they are not so clear. The brothers, on the other hand, are always clear—so Peter, James and John stayed home to sleep. They would have said to Mary, "It's foolish to go so early to the sepulchre! Why don't you stay home and sleep?" In the church life the sisters are always, in a sense, doing things foolishly. But I tell you, we do need many foolish sisters in the church life. It was through these foolish sisters that the resurrection of Christ was discovered. The Lord's first appearance was not to the clear brothers, but to the foolish sisters. What can we say? I don't think the Lord would appear to the clear Christians, but many, many times He does appear to the foolish ones. It is indisputable. The sisters were undoubtedly foolish, but they saw the Lord. They sought the Lord in a foolish way, but we can thank the Lord that they were so foolish. Whenever we become so clear, we are through as far as the Lord is concerned.

The Lord has made me a brother, and I must be satisfied with His creation; but sometimes I say, "Lord, why did you make me a man? I would like to be a sister. As a man it is so easy to miss you, but as a foolish sister, I would see you, I would meet you. I wish that I could be a sister!" The first meeting the Lord Jesus held after His resurrection was with a few sisters—there were no brothers! That was the first meeting of the New Testament with the resurrected Christ.

RESURRECTION MEETINGS

Now notice what the Lord said to Mary. "Go unto my brethren, and say to them, I ascend unto my Father and your Father, and my God and your God" (20:17). The Lord did not speak much with her; He gave her no long message. There was absolutely nothing religious in that contact. Suppose we were Jesus: we would probably say, "Mary, let us bow our heads and pray. Then let us sing a hymn and open to Psalm 16, where I will show you how I should rise from the dead." Then surely we would say, "Now Mary, since you have learned everything, go and tell my disciples. I will stand with you. I will pray for you. God be with you." But Jesus never did anything like this. He said one or two sentences that's all. No prayer, no singing, no Bible reading, no message, no promises of standing with you. This was what happened early in the morning.

Then in the evening of the same day, the disciples were in an extremely unsettled condition. Some like Mary had seen the Lord after His resurrection and had brought the news to the others. Some had seen the Lord during the day on the road to Emmaus. They came together not knowing where to turn or what to expect next. Suddenly the Lord Jesus was there. All the doors were shut, but Jesus suddenly appeared. There was nothing formal, nothing religious, nothing arranged, nothing scheduled. It simply says that Jesus came and stood in the midst and said unto them, "Peace be unto you." Again there was no prayer, no singing, no Bible reading, no God bless you, no "I'm standing with you"—no such thing. Just "Peace be unto you." After saying this, He did a very foolish thing to our natural mind. He breathed upon them. Jesus breathed into His disciples and said unto them, "Receive ye the Holy Spirit [or we may say, as in Greek, the Holy Breath]" (v. 22). Then, after breathing upon them, He said that they would be authorized either to forgive people or hold them sinful. That was all—that was absolutely all! What is this? It is certainly nothing religious. And there is no record that Jesus left. The record only says that Jesus came in when the doors were shut; it does not mention His leaving.

Then we read that after eight days, the disciples were together again and Jesus was in the midst (v. 26). Jesus came in again and again. The Bible records His coming in, but not His leaving. It is marvelous! What does all this mean? There was a meeting, in a sense, but never a dismissal. There was no one who said, "Let us be dismissed." We just read of the coming of the Lord Jesus, not His leaving. I believe the Lord is revealing something to us which is absolutely different from today's Christianity.

Do you not believe that what is recorded of those two evenings in John 20 were meetings, real meetings? They were undoubtedly meetings of the disciples with the resurrected Jesus. But according to our present realization there was no prayer there, no singing of hymns, no Bible reading, no message, and no dismissal. There was the coming in of Jesus, but not the going out. There was the start, but not the ending. Hallelujah!

MIRACLES AT THE SEA

Following chapter 20, we have a "P.S.," an appendix, showing us that those disciples were more or less like us. It may have been easy for them to go on in such a seemingly unsettled condition for a couple of days, but for them to continue longer than that was beyond their capacity. The time came, I do believe, when they had nothing more to eat. The leading brother, Peter, could stand it no longer. He said in effect, "Brothers, I'm going fishing, I'm going to get something to eat." All the others said, "Okay, if you go, we're going too." So they all went fishing and toiled drearily through the night. The right time for fishing is not during the day, but at night. So they fished at the right time. Furthermore, some of them were professional fishers, and not only that, but professional fishers on that very lake. Peter, James and John grew up there. They knew the lake from end to end, from side to side. Yet through the whole night they caught nothing. This was the greatest miracle! Could you believe that professional fishers fishing all night in a sea which they knew so well could catch nothing? Don't you think this is a miracle? The Lord Jesus must have told the fish, "Get away fish! All kinds of fish, take My order, stay away from My disciples till I tell you to come back." That was indeed a miracle. It was absolutely contrary to natural law.

Then the morning came. They should have been more than disappointed. If they could catch nothing in the night, how could they catch anything in the day? But in the midst of their despair the Lord Jesus came. He knew their problem—it was a matter of eating. So He asked,

"Children, have ye aught to eat?" (v. 5). They answered, "No!" Then the Lord replied, "Cast the net on the right side of the boat, and ye shall find." He said in effect, "Do it My way; do it according to My word." And they did. The daytime was not the right time to fish, but this time they fished according to the Lord's word. They got a net full of fishes, one hundred and fifty-three. Another miracle! And then when Peter came to land, he saw that the Lord had some fish there already. The Lord's implication to Peter was, "There is no need for you to go to sea to fish; even on land I can prepare fish for you. Peter and John, do you need fish? Why don't you ask Me? I am much better than the sea. Even if you go to sea, without My permission you can get nothing. If you only ask Me, though you stay at home, you will have all the fish you need."

Miracle number one was that they caught nothing for the whole night. Miracle number two was that in the morning, during the day, they caught so many fish. Miracle number three was that without catching anything from the sea, there was fish already on the land, and it was already cooked, and not only fish, but bread. It is marvelous! Everything is ready. Come and dine!

If we put all these points together, we will see that what the Lord said and did to the disciples, including Peter, gives a clear view of the church life today. The church life must be absolutely outside of religion. With religion, there is always a schedule, an organization, a system, an arrangement. But here there is none. There is only one thing, one living Person. And this One is always with us. In the open air or under a roof, indoors or outdoors, at home or at the seashore, He is always there. You simply cannot get rid of Him. Whether you are conscious or unconscious of His presence, He is always with you, and whatever you need He knows. If you need to eat, He will care for you. Don't go fishing—He has the fish. Just enjoy it. When problems arise, religion, as we have seen, uses the power of money. But the Lord Jesus exercises His universal authority. Whenever a work is started for the Lord, the natural, religious concept is always to consider the funds on hand. That was why Peter went fishing—it was the way to make money for eating. He felt that he at least needed something to buy groceries.

I do believe many young ones are burning to serve the Lord with their full time. Some have been hindered from doing so by the thought of the difficulty they will have in obtaining a living. But let me tell you that whenever we think anything about the matter of making a living, we are religious. With the living Jesus, with the resurrected Christ, there is no problem of making a living. Even without the sea, even on the land, if we need fish, the fish will be there. It all depends upon whether or not the Lord Jesus is with us. If we have the resurrected Christ with us, we may forget about all religious schedules and also about our living. The living Jesus not only cares for our spiritual need, but also for our physical need. He is not a dead religion; He is not a dead mission board. He is the living Christ. All the fishes are under His command.

According to the record of the four Gospels, Peter learned three lessons throughout his life from fishing. The first is recorded in Luke 5:1-11, where Peter was called by the Lord. At that time he caught a multitude of fish at Jesus' word. The second instance is recorded in Matthew 17:24-27, where Peter was told by the Lord to go fishing and find the tribute money in the fish's mouth. Now in John 21 we have the third instance. I am so thankful that we never read of Peter going back to fishing again.

Typically speaking, the day in which we are living is in the night. All night we must be kept from any religious attempt, any religious way of carrying on the Lord's work. Don't count your dollars. Don't look into your bank account. Don't estimate how many fishes you will need.

Last summer we had a large conference here in Los Angeles. The responsible ones knew nothing about schedules or budgets and did not calculate what they were going to spend beforehand. After it was over, I asked them concerning the conference account. I knew that we had spent much. Eventually we discovered that every need was fully met with a surplus remaining. Praise the Lord for that lesson. You see, this is the living Jesus, not a dead religion. This is Christ, not anything scheduled in a religious way.

Everything recorded in John 21 is undoubtedly with a purpose. Chapter 21 cannot compare, in a sense, with chapters 14 through 17 of John. But in another sense it is such a worthy and meaningful chapter. I am so grateful to the Lord for it now. I cannot tell you how much I love John 21. It is so practical and unreligious.

LOVING, FEEDING, FOLLOWING

After the disciples dined on the meal Jesus prepared, the Lord said to Peter, "Simon, son of John, lovest thou me more than these?" (v. 15). In effect, the Lord was saying to Peter, "A few days ago you said that though all others should deny me, you would not. But you did, and you did it three times; so I must ask you three times also, 'Do you love Me more than all the others?' " Peter replied, "Yea, Lord; thou knowest that I love thee." What he may have meant was this: "Lord, I really don't know whether I love You or not. You know. And even if I did know, I would not dare to say it. Just a few days ago I said that I would never deny You, but immediately afterwards I did. Whatever I say doesn't count, but whatever You know really counts. Lord, You know that I love You." Peter was not sure exactly how to answer. But this is not the point. Listen! The Lord said to Peter, "Feed my lambs." Then the second time the Lord told him, "Tend my sheep." And then the third time, "Feed my sheep." The Lord did not tell him to teach or instruct, or even to edify, but just to feed. Our love for the Lord must issue in our feeding of His lambs. Finally, the Lord Jesus gave Peter one additional word, "Follow me" (vv. 19, 22).

I say this especially to the young brothers and sisters—love the Lord Jesus, feed His lambs, and follow Him. That is good enough. Nothing else is required. True service to the Lord consists of loving Him, feeding His lambs, and following Him. And where is He? He is in our spirit. We must follow Him in our spirit. We must exercise our heart to love Him—to love is a heart matter (Mark 12:30). But to follow the Lord is a matter of the spirit, for the Lord today is in our spirit (I Cor. 6:17). We must simply love Him with our heart and follow Him by exercising our spirit; then we will be nourished by Him. With the nourishment by which we are nourished, we may then feed His lambs. This is absolutely nothing of religion. Don't think that you need to know the Bible, go to seminary or Bible college, and receive a religious education. You don't need that. You need the first, best, and genuine love for the Lord Jesus. The Lord asked Peter, "Lovest thou me more than these?" We must answer, "Yea, Lord; Thou knowest that I love Thee." The service of the Lord in this New Testament dispensation is not a matter of knowledge or education, but absolutely a matter of loving the Lord. The degradation of the church began with the loss of this—"I have this against thee, that thou didst leave thy first love" (Rev. 2:4). As long as we have the first, best, and genuine love for the Lord, we are safe. Then we must follow Him who is in our spirit. We love Him with all our heart, and we follow Him by our spirit; then whatever we do is just to feed His lambs. Praise the Lord!

Now you may realize where we should stand and where we must stand. We have the Lord Jesus, the resurrected, living One meeting with us all the time—anywhere, everywhere, anytime, everytime, without any schedule, plan or arrangement. He is everything to us. All we need to do is simply to love Him with all our hearts and follow Him by our spirit, thus obtaining the nourishment to feed others.

COMMISSIONED FROM THE MOUNTAIN

At the end of both Matthew and John we see a further matter which is quite significant. At the end of Matthew, Jesus met with His disciples in a place appointed by Him, a mountain top. Mountains in the Bible always signify something higher with authority for God's kingdom. This is why the Lord Jesus, on the mountain appointed by Him, told His disciples that all authority both in heaven and on earth has been given unto Him. In so saying He passed on this authority to His disciples and said unto them, "Go ye therefore." The word "therefore" means that the authority which has been given unto Him has now been given unto us, and with this authority we are told to go and disciple the nations. This is not merely the preaching of the Gospel, but an exercise and execution of the authority given to the Lord Jesus both in heaven and on earth. It is not the propagating of a low-standard Gospel, delivering people from hell and bringing them to heaven, but a discipling of the nations, baptizing them into the name of the triune God. Many times while referring to certain people we say, "They have the name, but they do not have the reality." In our human concept we separate the name from the reality. But in the Bible the name is the reality. To baptize people into the name of the Father and of the Son and of the Holy Spirit means to baptize them into the reality of the triune God. That is our commission. We must disciple the heathen (the word "nations" can be translated "heathen") and put them into the reality of the all-inclusive God. The issue then will eventually be the kingdom of heaven; and in the kingdom, as priests, we must teach them to observe all things whatsoever He has commanded us—this is to teach them how to be citizens of the heavenly kingdom. Then the Lord Jesus says in effect that since the kingdom of heaven is among us, He will be with us all the days until the completion of this age.

The risen Christ today is on this earth in a way to commission us with His authority, that we may bear the responsibility to disciple the heathen and put them into the reality of the triune God. Thus the kingdom of the heavens is established on this earth. And then we have the assurance that this Jesus, this God-man, this Redeemer, this risen One, this all-inclusive Christ, is with us.

You see how far removed this is from religion. Do you really believe that such a Christ is with you today? If so, you will be more than excited and burdened with His commission. We all need to be beside ourselves with this—so much so that we can go into the streets and lay hold of people, telling them, "Friends, you must realize that Jesus is with me, the resurrected Christ is with me, the Christ who holds all authority both in heaven and on earth." Have you ever been so crazy? I'm afraid that you are too religious and dumb. If you have Christ with you, how can you be so silent?

In Matthew 28 it was the disciples who preceded the Lord Jesus to the mountain. "The eleven disciples went into Galilee, unto the mountain where Jesus had appointed them" (v. 16). They went to the mountain which the Lord Jesus had appointed, and eventually the Lord came. It was not the Lord who was waiting for them, but they who were waiting for the Lord. They were really high at that time.

But after Matthew 28, we come to John 21. Their high didn't last very long; they came down from the mountain. I must confess that I like John 21 much better than Matthew 28, because according to my experience I am not always so high. Many times I am not in Matthew 28, but John 21. In Matthew 28 we have a mountain, while in John 21 we have the seashore. Where are you in your experience now—on the mountain or on the seashore? If you are honest, most of you will admit that you are presently on the seashore. The seashore in John 21 was not so good; it was not the place appointed by the Lord. The Lord appointed a mountain, not the seashore. The sea was a place to which the disciples backslid. Peter took the lead, and they all went to the sea—it was their choice.

The fishing in John 21 does not have positive significance, but negative. If you have come to this country just
to make a living, if you are in any place merely for your
living, that is the fishing mentioned in John 21. You don't
care for the Lord's commission; you only care for your
living. The Lord commissioned you in Matthew 28, but
you couldn't stand the test, you gave up His commission
to care for your living. You said like Peter, "I go a fishing."

For people to make a living is according to the natural
law. God created man, and man must live; so God has
prepared the things for man's living. To make a living is
all right; but as a child of God, a disciple of Jesus
commissioned with His authority, we should not be here
for our living. Are you? We must be here for the Lord's
commission in Matthew 28. We must not be here for
fishing, but for "churching."

We have already seen how the disciples fished through
the entire night and caught nothing. Then when morning
came, the Lord Jesus was there. It is quite interesting.
In Matthew on the mountaintop, the disciples were
waiting for the Lord, but here on the seashore the Lord
Jesus was waiting for them. I do believe that when Peter
and the others went to the sea, the Lord was there already.
He was always with them. Whether they were in a
building or in the open air, whether they were on the
mountaintop or at the seashore, wherever they were, He
was there. When they were casting the net, He was there
also. In fact, He was managing the situation so that they
caught nothing. It was not under their hand, but Jesus'.
And then He manifested Himself to them and showed that
He had the food prepared and it was already cooked.

If we do mean business that we are here for the Lord's
commission, the Lord will take care of our living. Everyone
may be jobless, but we will still have bread. People today
are so greatly concerned about the unemployment problem, but we may forget it. That has nothing to do with
us; we are not here for making a living. Whether fish can
be caught or not, we don't depend on the sea. We depend

on the living Christ; He has all the fish in His hand. The
worldly people do not have Christ; they must depend on
the sea. But not us. If you are one who is for the world,
you must be concerned for your living, you must put your
trust in your employment. But if you are one of the
disciples commissioned by the Lord Jesus, forget about
your living. Just be honest and faithful to His commission.
You will even save your cooking. The Lord said, "Come
and dine." Don't worry about eating—He will take care
of that.

COMMISSIONED AT THE SEASHORE

We have seen how the Lord selected Peter and
questioned him three times concerning his love. The Lord
said in effect, "You go fishing more than all the rest do
you love me more than all the rest?" And then He spoke
to him with this implication, "Just as I have fed you here
with fish and bread, so you must feed My lambs and My
sheep. You are not on this earth for fishing—you are
commissioned on this earth for shepherding." Matthew
precedes and John follows. The sequence is absolutely
right. We need Matthew 28, and we also need John 21.
John 21 is a supplementary portion, giving us the
completion of the Lord's commission. The Lord has
commissioned us not only to disciple the heathen, baptizing them into the reality of the triune God and setting
up the kingdom of the heavens on this earth, but also to
shepherd His flock. We must feed the little lambs and
even the sheep. The Lord is speaking to us, "You take
care of My flock; I will take care of your living. You leave
the matter of living to Me. I need you to shepherd My
flock."

My burden is to share that the Lord Jesus today has
a real commission for us, not a religion. Today, even in
the U.S.A. how many heathen there are! What they need
is not a religion, but a group of people who will realize
and execute the Lord's commission. Please do not read
Matthew chapter 28 as an historical record. It is not a

history; it is a commission. We all must be burdened by
the Lord to disciple the heathen and put them into the
triune God, setting up the kingdom of the heavens even
here on this earth. But there is also the need of John 21.
Without John 21, Matthew 28 will not work so well. After
you disciple the heathen, after you baptize them into the
reality of the triune God, after the kingdom is set up, the
flock still needs to be fed and shepherded. I do have a
heavy burden for so many young ones and new ones. Who
is going to feed them? Shall we hire graduates from the
seminary? Are the leading brothers in the churches going
to tend to this? No! The whole church must do it. We are
all commissioned. On one hand we must disciple the
heathen and make them citizens of the kingdom of heaven
on this earth. Then, on the other hand, we must consider
them the lambs, the little ones, the weaker ones in the
kingdom, who need feeding. We must feed them. This is
not just the responsibility of the leading ones, but of every
member in the local churches. We all must bear the
burden. I'm so happy for the increase in the churches, but
I'm also very much concerned for the increase. If this
matter of feeding is not accomplished in a full way, the
increase will be a heavy burden to the church life. Instead
of going up, the church life will go down. There is an
urgent need that we be charged not only with Matthew
28, but also with John 21, not only to disciple the heathen,
but also to feed the lambs.

To disciple the heathen we need the authority, but to
feed the lambs, we need the love towards the Lord. In
Matthew 28, the Lord's tone was one of authority, and
with that He charged the disciples. But in John 21 His
tone is changed. "Simon, son of John, lovest thou me more
than these?" If so, "Feed my lambs." Don't exercise your
authority over the lambs. If you do that, you will frighten
them away. You must love them, not with your love, but
with the love with which you love the Lord Jesus. Why
should you feed the younger ones and care for the weaker
ones? Simply because you love the Lord Jesus. If we really

love Him, there is no other way but to feed others. And by doing this, we follow Him. We must follow Him not in the way of religion, but in the way of feeding His lambs till He comes back.

Matthew says, "Be charged, be commissioned to disciple the nations until the completion of this age." John says, "Love the Lord, feed His lambs, and follow Him till He returns." It is really good. In what way may we prove our love for the Lord Jesus? Feed His lambs. Feed His sheep. And this is the proper way for us to follow Him.

We remember how Peter turned and saw John and said to the Lord, "What shall this man do?" The Lord Jesus answered him, "Forget about him. That's My business, not yours. You just follow Me." We should not care what others will do; we must make a personal and direct deal with the Lord ourselves.

The Lord Jesus met with His disciples on the mountaintop and at the seashore, in the place which He appointed and at the place to which they backslid. Regardless, He met with them to fulfill His purpose, and in both places they enjoyed His presence in a full way. On the mountaintop He committed to them His all-inclusive authority beyond their understanding. On the seashore He cared for all their needs beyond their expectation. On the mountaintop He commissioned them to disciple the nations, baptizing them into the triune God. On the seashore He challenged Peter to love Him, charged Him to feed His lambs and sheep, and bade him follow Him to the end of his life. In all these dealings of the resurrected Christ, we can see nothing in the nature of any kind of religion. All the Lord in resurrection would do is to commission us with His authority to bring people into God and demand that we love Him that we may be burdened to feed His flock, thus following Him to the end of our life journey. This is all we need today in His recovery—to share His authority, to disciple the heathen by baptizing them into God, to love Him more than others, to feed His lambs and sheep, and to follow Him at any cost, even at the cost of our life, regardless of what others shall do. This is to experience the resurrected Christ, to minister Him to others and to share Him with others. It is altogether a matter of Christ and Christ alone, nothing at all of religion.

CHAPTER TEN

CHRIST VERSUS RELIGION IN THE BOOK OF ACTS

Scripture Reading: Acts 4:1-3, 5-7, 13, 18-21; 5:17-29, 33, 40-41; 6:9-13; 7:54-59; 8:1-3; 9:1-5; 10:9-16; 11:1-3, 12, 19; 15:1-2, 28-29; 21:17-28

CHRIST IS ONE WITH THE SAINTS

We all must realize that in the Book of Acts Christ is living with all His members. Never think that Christ is only in the four Gospels and not in the Acts. In the Gospels we have Christ in the body given Him by Mary, His physical body; but in the Acts we have Christ in a larger Body, a mystical Body, given Him by the Holy Spirit. Acts 1 tells how Christ ascended into the heavens in the presence of all His followers. Then Acts 2 tells how this ascended Christ came down upon His followers. From that day, the Day of Pentecost, Christ was fully one with all His saints. From that day He was not only within them, but also upon them; He not only filled them, but also clothed them. He was fully and thoroughly one with all His disciples to the extent that His disciples just became Jesus Christ.

You remember what that persecutor, Saul of Tarsus, heard when he was smitten down on the road to Damascus: The Lord Jesus said to him, "Saul, Saul, why persecutest thou Me?" (Acts 9:4). Then Saul replied in so many words, "Lord, who are You? I never persecuted anyone in the heavens; all those whom I persecuted were on earth. I persecuted John, I persecuted Peter, and I persecuted Stephen; now I am on my way to persecute

some people in the city of Damascus. Who are You?" The
Lord Jesus answered, "I am Jesus whom thou persecutest."
The Lord said in effect, "You must realize that Peter, John,
Stephen, and all My believers are just Me. When you
persecute them, you persecute Me. I am one with them,
and they are one with Me."

Hence, in the Book of Acts Christ is still here on this
earth living with, in, and among all His disciples. We all
must realize that the sufferings, journeys, and speeches
of these disciples were absolutely the acts of Jesus. Jesus
was still acting, living, moving, working, and doing things
in all His disciples.

CHRIST, THE TARGET OF RELIGION

We can also see in the Book of Acts that Christ was
still versus religion. The battle between Christ and
religion was even more severe in the Book of Acts than
in the four Gospels. The disciples of Jesus went forward
testifying and witnessing for Jesus, absolutely ignoring
religion. This greatly offended the religious people and
rulers; therefore, they exercised their religious authority
to arrest and imprison them. The religious rulers, in a
sense, were opposing all the followers of Jesus, but they
were not mainly against the followers, but against Jesus
Himself. They had no problem with those Galilean
followers of Jesus; their problem was with Jesus. They
instructed the disciples never to speak or teach in the
name of Jesus. You see, they didn't mind their teaching
or preaching as long as they would leave out the name of
Jesus. They were not against those Galileans; they were
against Jesus. They did not hate His followers; they hated
Jesus. The disciples, of course, would not take their word:
they had something more living and powerful within them
than what they heard from those religious rulers. They
proceeded fearlessly to preach and to praise Christ, and
thus brought upon themselves swift arrest and imprison-
ment.

But that was not the end. "An angel of the Lord by
night opened the prison doors, and brought them out, and

said, Go ye, and stand and speak in the temple to the people all the words of this life" (5:19-20). What life? The life which nothing can hold, the life which even the prison cannot hold. The angel told them to go and speak the words of such a life. And so they went early in the morning to the temple and spoke. The rulers sent the officers to the prison that day to bring forth the disciples to the counsel, and the officers returned saying, "The prison house we found shut in all safety, and the keepers standing at the doors: but when we had opened, we found no man within" (v. 23). Eventually, they found all the prisoners in the temple speaking boldly in the name of Jesus. When the chief priests received this report, we read that they were "much perplexed concerning them whereunto this would grow" (v. 24). They probably said one to another, "What shall we do? We cannot do anything with these people." What they really meant was that they could not do anything with this life. The Galilean people were nothing, but the life within them was tremendous. The life was the real troublemaker, not those Galilean fishermen.

Then in chapter 6 various groups of people came to debate with Stephen. Have you noticed what kind of people they were? They were the people of all the synagogues, of all the various groups of religion from different places. All combined to fight against Stephen. Eventually, outwardly speaking, they gained the victory because they stoned Stephen to death; but inwardly they lost the case. We must realize that Stephen was not there by himself. While they were stoning him, he was connected to the heavens. At that very moment "the heavens opened," and Stephen saw "the Son of man standing on the right hand of God." That means that Jesus was one with Stephen, and Stephen was one with Jesus. That also means that the heavens and the earth, the earth and the heavens, were also one. They were not persecuting Stephen; they were persecuting Jesus. They were not stoning Stephen; they were stoning Jesus who had ascended to the heavens. It is not a small matter.

SAUL,
A HORSE IN JESUS' CHARIOT

When Saul of Tarsus witnessed Stephen's martyrdom, he was wholly for it. He gave himself utterly to stamp out this Jesus. Stephen's stoning, he thought, was a great victory, and now he could press the persecution even further. Therefore, he went to the chief priest, requesting authority to bind and imprison all those in Damascus who called on this Name. We all know the story: while he was on his way, Jesus spoke from heaven—the One who saw Stephen stoned to death, the One who was one with Stephen, now came to visit this persecutor. A little light came from the heavens and Saul was smitten to the ground. "Saul, Saul, why persecutest thou Me?" The Lord Jesus spoke very nicely to Saul—have you noticed this? "I am Jesus whom thou persecutest." "It is hard for thee to kick against the pricks." The Lord's words were very meaningful. In the ancient times there were pricks or goads on the carriages to keep the horses in check. Sometimes the horses would kick and rebel against the carriage and their driver. When they did, they were pricked by the goads and thus given a lesson. To the Lord Jesus, what Saul was doing was kicking against the pricks. The Lord said to Saul in so many words, "Saul, regardless of how much you are persecuting Me, you are still under My rule. I am riding you; you are not riding Me. You are a horse in My carriage, and you are not being a good horse. Stop your kicking. You are kicking the pricks, and you can never succeed. You see, now you have landed on the ground." Then Saul's inner eyes began to open. He probably began to reason with himself, "Oh, it's not so good for me to persecute this Jesus. This Jesus is not so small; this Jesus is great, both in heaven and on earth. I am under the rule of this Jesus whom I have been persecuting: I am just a little horse, and He's doing the riding." This persecutor was marvelously subdued. The Lord Jesus gained the victory over the scribes, over the Sadducees, over the Pharisees, over the chief priests, and even over this persecutor. The Lord gained the victory over all the religious people.

RELIGIOUS PETER

Now when we come to chapter 10, we see that the Lord Jesus had a problem, not with the priests, not with the Pharisees, not with the persecutors, but with Peter. Up to Acts 10 Peter was still more or less religious. In Acts 2, 3, 4, and 5 Peter appeared marvelous, heavenly, absolutely out of religion and wholly in the spirit; but when we come to chapter 10, we see another Peter, a religious Peter. Peter went to the rooftop to pray according to a certain time schedule. That was not bad: I do not blame anyone for praying according to a time schedule— sometimes we need to do this. But have you realized that at that time Peter was still religious? Peter did not realize it. Suddenly, in a kind of trance, he saw something descend from the heavens which was diametrically opposed to his religious concept. I cannot tell, of course, what Peter was praying at the moment of this unexpected vision. It is quite probable, however, that he was praying for all the Jews to be converted, for all his countrymen to be saved. He may have been asking the Lord to send a great revival upon the Jewish nation. But while he was faithfully keeping the hour of prayer, he suddenly saw a vessel let down from heaven, wherein were "all manner of four-footed beasts and creeping things of the earth and birds of the heaven" (v. 12). Then came the Lord's word, "Rise, Peter; kill and eat" (v. 13). This shocked Peter. What he heard was absolutely contrary to the law and to the Scripture in Leviticus chapter 11. The children of Israel were only allowed to eat the clean animals, not the unclean. But here were all kinds of living creatures, and the Lord was asking him to eat them. By reading the context of these verses carefully, we see the probability of every creature in that great sheet being unclean. In any case, it was full of unclean things. The Lord told him to "kill and eat," but Peter said, "Not so, Lord; for I have never eaten anything that is common and unclean." In other words, Peter said, "This is against my practice." He did not use the word "religion," but he meant that.

You have realized by now that we must get rid of religion, but have you realized that to get rid of religion is not so easy? Could you imagine that a person like Peter still retained to this point some amount of religion? Look at Peter in the opening chapters of Acts, and then look at him here in chapter 10. There is another person in this chapter, a person who is still caring for religion, neglecting the Spirit. Peter forced the Lord to speak three times to him, and still he did not understand. Then when the Gentiles from Cornelius came seeking Peter, the Spirit within him told him to go.

PETER LEARNS HIS LESSON

This time Peter remembered well the lesson he learned with such difficulty in Matthew 17. You remember how the Lord Jesus brought James and John together with Peter to the mount of transfiguration, but Peter did not consult with them; Peter did not care for them. This time, however, Peter remembered. When the men from Cornelius came and the Spirit bade him go with them, he took six other brethren. On the mount of transfiguration he had only two brothers, James and John; but this time he took six brothers with him. Seven brothers went as one to visit Cornelius. There was no more individualism—Peter had learned the lesson. He could no more act individualistically; he was quite careful about this. In this matter Peter was religiously wrong, but so spiritually right. The Lord never told Peter to take six brothers with him; the Lord never gave him this kind of command. But Peter was on the alert: he realized that if he went to the Gentiles he would certainly be put on the spot by all his Jewish brothers. Therefore, he took these brothers not only to be his witnesses, but also as his protection. That was really good. Peter took it upon himself to do this. Sometimes we must do something which the Lord Jesus has never told us to do. There are instances when to do something which He has not commanded will please the Lord even more than doing that which He has told us to do.

Then they went to Cornelius—you know the story. While Peter was speaking to them, the Holy Spirit came down upon the Gentiles exactly as He did upon the Jewish believers on the Day of Pentecost. All the brothers who accompanied Peter saw it. Then when they returned to Jerusalem, just as Peter had suspected, all his Jewish brethren asked, "How come?" They said in effect, "Peter, you went to a Gentile home; you had fellowship with Gentiles. How come?" What is this? This again is religion. Not to eat anything unclean was religious, and not to contact the unclean Gentiles was again religious. Religion was still with them and was quite prevailing. But Peter had gotten the vision, and he stood and rehearsed the whole matter from beginning to end. He said, "I was not the only one who saw the Holy Spirit descend upon the Gentiles. These six brothers were with me—they saw it too." Two, you know, is always the number for testimony; but now Peter had three times two. Peter learned the lesson so well in Matthew 17 that he could never forget. The Lord brought only two to the mountaintop with Peter, but now Peter took three times that many with him to visit Cornelius. Praise the Lord. Peter really learned his lesson. Thus, in chapter 11, he could speak so strongly, "Don't blame me. If I am wrong, the six brothers are wrong also. They all went with me—what can you say?" Seven is the number of completion. Seven brothers stood together against religion. Isn't this good!

The point is this: religion is within our blood. Peter was outside of religion, but religion was still in him, and not only in him, but in so many Jewish believers. They had seen how the Lord Jesus did everything outside of religion, but there was still an amount of religion within them. I'm still concerned that within so many of us, after seeing so clearly the nature of religion, there is still a certain amount of religion. The time will come when you will be tested and you will say, "Not so, Lord; throughout all my Christian life I have never done that."

THE CONFERENCE IN JERUSALEM
CONCERNING RELIGION

Following chapters 10 and 11, we come to chapter 15, where we read that certain men went down to Antioch from Jerusalem telling the people, "Except ye be circumcised after the custom of Moses, ye cannot be saved" (v. 1). Listen to the religion. How religious can you be! Yet they were believers. In so short a time after chapters 2, 3, 4 and 5 of Acts, we see how so many Jewish believers returned to religion. A great stir was created among the churches in the Gentile world; so the elders decided to send Paul and Barnabas to Jerusalem about this matter. At the conference in Jerusalem, by the mercy of the Lord, the decision was made not to perpetuate such teaching. Praise the Lord for that.

To leave our religious background is really difficult. If there were no background, it would be easy. The situation today is exactly the same: we do have a religious background, and almost every one of us has come out of it. The problem is that we have come out of it, but it has not come out of us. We have said to religion, "I divorce you," but religion has said to us, "I will never leave you." Brothers and sisters, please do not read this chapter on the behalf of others; read it for yourself. It is easy to get out of religion, but it is not easy to get religion out of us.

PAUL'S PROBLEM
WITH RELIGION

The Apostle Paul, we know, wrote the Epistles to the Galatians and the Romans, in which he spoke so strongly against anything of the old religion. Could you imagine that after writing these two books, when Paul went up to Jerusalem, he would be convinced to perform a ritualistic act in the Jewish temple? Yet he did. It is recorded in Acts chapter 21. And he was persuaded to do this by no less than the elders of the church. Let us read this portion again—it is amazing.

"And when we were come to Jerusalem, the brethren
received us gladly. And the day following Paul went
in with us unto James; and all the elders were
present. And when he had saluted them, he rehearsed one by one the things which God had
wrought among the Gentiles through his ministry.
And they, when they heard it, glorified God."

This is really good! Hallelujah! But it was not so simple.

"And they said unto him, Thou seest, brother, how many
thousands there are among the Jews of them that
have believed; and they are all zealous for the law:
and they have been informed concerning thee, that
thou teachest all the Jews who are among the
Gentiles to forsake Moses, telling them not to
circumcise their children neither to walk after the
custom."

That was absolutely correct—Paul did this. Read the
Book of Galatians, read the Book of Romans; Paul really
did this.

"What is it therefore? They will certainly hear that
thou art come. Do therefore this that we say to
thee..."

The elders, listen, the elders were speaking to Paul.

"We have four men that have a vow on them; these take,
and purify thyself with them, and be at charges
for them, that they may shave their heads: and all
shall know that there is no truth in the things
whereof they have been informed concerning thee;
but that thou thyself also walkest orderly, keeping
the law. But as touching the Gentiles that have
believed, we wrote, giving judgment that they
should keep themselves from things sacrificed to
idols, and from blood, and from what is strangled,
and from fornication. Then Paul took the men, and
the next day purifying himself with them went into
the temple, declaring the fulfillment of the days of

purification, until the offering was offered for every
one of them" (Acts 21:17-26).

Could you believe that Paul would do this? O Lord
Jesus, O Lord Jesus, be merciful to us! Could you believe
that by the time of Acts 21 all the elders in Jerusalem
would give Paul such advice? They were not the small
brothers, but the elders, including James. Their advice in
effect was this: "We have decided not to ask the Gentile
believers to keep the law, but we the Jews still need to
keep the law." Perhaps Paul in taking their advice felt
that he should "become all things to all men" (I Cor. 9:22).
Perhaps this was his reasoning. But regardless of how
much we try to excuse our brother Paul, the Lord Jesus
would not agree, and the Lord would not honor what he
did. Let us read verse 27: "And when the seven days [for
the ritual of purification] were almost completed, the Jews
from Asia, when they saw him in the temple, stirred up
all the multitude and laid hands on him, crying out, Men
of Israel, help: this is the man that teacheth all men
everywhere against the people, and the law, and this place;
and moreover he brought Greeks also into the temple..."
The Lord couldn't take it any longer; He allowed some
people to interfere with the ritual before it was accomplished. It was by this that Paul was put into prison, where
he remained until his death. And it was not long after this
that the Lord sent the Roman Army under Titus in 70
A.D. to destroy the temple, Jerusalem, and the Jewish
religion. The Jewish elders said, "Thou seest, brother, how
many thousands there are among the Jews of them that
have believed; and they are all zealous for the law." But
it seems that the Lord was saying, "I will send an army
to wipe out the whole thing." And He did. That was the
end, hallelujah, that was the end! Praise the Lord, since
that time we can find no record in history of any elders
giving the brothers such advice. Everything was wiped out.

THE ROOT OF RELIGION IN US

Let me warn you again of thinking that you are

through with religion. I tell you, you may be through with religion, but religion will not be through with you. You may have decided to divorce your "wife," but your "dear wife" will never leave you. This religious wife is a real wife; it is really difficult for anyone to get rid of her.

Several years ago some brothers from a certain place learned to pray-read and then returned to their meeting with other believers to practice it. A general cry of alarm arose and it reached my ears. "Oh, oh, we cannot take this! The people here are not used to this!" This again was the story of religion. They reacted just as Peter did when the Lord let down the sheet from heaven. "Not so Lord; for I have never eaten anything that is common and unclean." But the Lord said, "What God hath cleansed, make not thou common." The Lord said in other words, "You may not like it, but I like it." Eventually, the Lord gained the victory in that place.

Shall we limit the Lord? Who knows what the Lord will do and how far the Lord will go. I am not fighting for pray-reading, shouting, or loud praising, but I am saying that we must get rid of anything religious. You may say that you are not used to something new, but the Lord says, "Behold, I make all things new" (Rev. 21:5). What would you say? What can you say?

Peter did have the scriptural ground in the law not to eat anything unclean. But today we have no ground to maintain our old kind of Christian "service." We must confess that it is pure tradition. Peter's insistence not to eat anything unclean was fully grounded in the Old Testament Scriptures. But if today you say that you do not like loud shouting and praising in the meetings, you have no ground in the Bible, not one word. The Lord be merciful to us that we may be willing to drop all our religious concepts. You may say something is unclean, but the Lord says He has sanctified it. You may say you cannot contact the Gentiles, but the Lord says that He has chosen them before the foundation of the world. If you do not go to them, sooner or later you will meet them in the New Jerusalem. You will meet the people you despise face to face. Then what will you do? You say you do not like noisy meetings, but the Lord Jesus says He likes them. "I am so happy," He says, "that they are calling upon My name." O Lord Jesus! O Lord Jesus! O Lord Jesus!

Religion has become and still is a real pit to us. We have fallen into this pit. I do not mean that in throwing over religion we should be foolishly crazy. We should in the proper sense be sober. Yet it is easy to get out of religion, but not easy to get religion out of us. The Lord Jesus, when He was on earth, acted so clearly before His disciples, showing them by example His attitude toward religion. They all saw it; they were all made clear that Jesus would have nothing to do with religion. Furthermore, they were all clothed with the Lord Himself on the Day of Pentecost and became His bold and living witnesses. Yet in Acts chapter 10, chapter 15, and chapter 21, the root of religion still in them was exposed. It seems incredible to us, but we must consider ourselves. What about the root of religion still in us? The Lord be merciful to us.

Today, in principle, we are in the same situation. Christianity today is almost a religion. Don't think that since Christianity has the Bible, everything is well. Don't think that since Christianity today preaches Christ, everything is fine. In the ancient times the elders of Judaism had the Bible, and they also taught something about Christ. But Christ Himself was there, and they did not care for Him. It is exactly the same in principle today.

Dr. A. W. Tozer of recent years wrote an article shortly before his death in which the main point was this: Christianity today has its conferences in which they discuss Christian service, missionary endeavor, etc. But suppose Christ Himself should enter their conference room. They would ask Him, "Who are you?" So wrote the famous minister of the Christian Missionary Alliance, A. W. Tozer. This is today's Christianity. And this is not my word, but his.

We must be aware; we must be on the alert. Never think that just because someone has the Bible and preaches Christ, he is all right. We must all be so living with the living Christ, not with anything religious, not with anything of Christianity, not with anything of tradition, organization, regulation, forms, mere teachings, and dead doctrines. Christ is only Christ Himself, and Christ cares only for Himself; He does not care for a Christ in doctrine, a Christ in history, or the Christ in your mind. He only cares for Himself, the living Christ in your spirit. This is the day of the Lord's recovery, and this recovery is of the living Christ in our spirit. It has nothing to do with any forms, regulations, teachings or doctrines in dead letters. Oh, let us give ourselves to be one with this living Christ!

We have seen from the record of the Gospels how the Lord Jesus began to be opposed to religion in the matter of fasting. From fasting, He began to break through all the religious things. We have seen how He broke the keeping of the sabbath and put it aside. Then, in Acts 10, He broke the law of eating unclean things, and in so doing broke the law of separation from the Gentile world. Following this, the Lord broke the law of circumcision (Acts 15), and eventually He broke through the whole religion. He sent the Roman Army in 70 A.D. under Titus, the Prince of the Roman Empire, to utterly wipe out Judaism. May the Lord be merciful to bring us completely out of religion and to bring religion completely out of us.

CHAPTER ELEVEN

CHRIST VERSUS RELIGION
IN THE EPISTLES

Scripture Reading: Rom. 2:29; 7:6; II Cor. 3:6; Gal. 1:12-16; 2:1-5, 11-14; 5:1-4, 25; 6:15; Eph. 4:11-16; Phil. 3:2-14; Col. 2:8-9,16-17, 20-22; 3:11; Heb. 7:16.

In the verses which we have noted above, we have begun with Romans and ended with Hebrews. This means we have covered almost the entire section of the Epistles. In all these letters we will see how much Christ is versus religion.

IN ROMANS

In the letter to the Romans we have selected two verses, one in chapter 2 and one in chapter 7. In chapter 2 we read that what we need is nothing outwardly religious, but something inwardly in spirit. "But he is a Jew who is one inwardly; and circumcision is that of the heart, in the spirit not in the letter..." (v. 29). In other words, this verse tells us clearly that we should be in spirit, not just in the letter of the written Scriptures. This word is written by the Apostle Paul. Suppose there were not such a word in the Bible and I should say that you must be in the spirit and not care so much for the letter of the written Scriptures. I believe you would stone me to death. Hallelujah, Paul the Apostle took the lead. This is not my teaching; this is my quotation. I am just a little follower; the Apostle Paul is my protection. If you would stone anyone, you must stone him first. I do have scriptural ground to say that what we need is something in the spirit, not anything merely in the letter according to the written Scriptures. Who can argue? Please do not misunderstand me: I am not saying, nor have I ever said, that we should not care for the Scriptures. I am saying that we must have something in the spirit, not merely according to the letter of the written Scriptures. What we need is the living Christ, not merely the black and white letters of the written code. This is the principle of Christ versus religion.

We have seen that the very Christ whom we enjoy today is the life-giving Spirit indwelling our spirit, and that He, the life-giving Spirit, is made one with our spirit. "He that is joined unto the Lord is one spirit" (I Cor. 6:17). When we say that we need to be "in spirit," we mean in this wonderful, mingled spirit. In this spirit we have the Lord Jesus as the life-giving Spirit. Anything that is in spirit is Christ. Merely to be in the letter of the written Scriptures is to be religious. Those who are such do not care for Christ; they only care for the written code. We have seen in the four Gospels the living Christ standing before those religious people. But they only cared for the letter of their Scriptures. In John chapter 7, in Christ's very presence, they asked, "What, doth the Christ come out of Galilee? Hath not the scriptures said that the Christ cometh of the seed of David, and from Bethlehem" (vv. 41-42). On one hand they held their Bible, and on the other hand they were in the presence of the living Christ. They cared for their Bible, but not for the living Christ. Do you think the situation of today's Christianity is any different?

More than forty years ago I was with a group of Christians who spent much time with the Bible. I have never seen any like them who were so familiar with the letter of the Word. One among them was even called "the living concordance." At a certain time some among us began to have some living experience of Christ. We heard the Lord speaking within our spirit. When the news reached the leading one of that group, an old brother with extensive knowledge of the Bible, he was exceedingly surprised. He asked, "How could this be? God's Word from

Genesis to Revelation has been absolutely completed. If you would hear anything from God, you must study the Word. After completing the Bible, God never speaks to people any more." This was their concept. For anyone to hear a living word of God apart from studying the Bible was in their eyes as heresy. I was somewhat troubled by the attitude of such a leading and elderly brother. But something within strengthened me to such an extent that I not only testified, but proclaimed that it is absolutely proper for the Lord to speak to people today in the spirit. This kind of situation exposes the state of Christianity. They care for their Bible, but they do not care for Christ. They care for the doctrine concerning Christ, but they do not care for the living, instant Christ Himself.

Romans 7:6 says, "But now we have been discharged from the law, having died to that wherein we were held; so that we serve in newness of the spirit, and not in oldness of the letter." Now we know what the word "letter" here refers to—it is the written Bible. Today we must serve the living Lord with newness in the spirit, not according to the oldness of the written Bible. I can say this boldly, because I am a little follower of this most bold one, the Apostle Paul. Now we serve not according to the oldness of the written code, the written Bible, but according to the newness of the spirit. Why? Because in the spirit is Christ, while in the written code is religion. This is Christ versus religion.

What is it to be religious? To be religious is simply to be sound, scriptural, and fundamental, yet without the presence of Christ. If we lack His presence, regardless of how scriptural we are, we are simply religious. Paul in these two verses of Romans laid a solid foundation for Christ versus religion. Today our service, our work, and even our life must be altogether in the spirit, not merely according to the letters of the written Bible. I know that when I say this I run a risk. I will be charged with the heresy of turning people away from the Bible. But I simply refer you to these two passages of Scripture, Romans 2:29 and Romans 7:6. Everyone must admit that the word "letter" in these passages refers to the written Scriptures. There can be no argument. Christ is versus religion; Christ is versus the written code. We may have the right quotation from the written code, yet miss Christ, just as the Pharisees and scribes in ancient times. We must be alert not to pay that much attention to the written code. If we do, it is altogether possible and extremely probable that we will miss Christ. The only way of safety is to behold "with unveiled face the glory of the Lord" (II Cor. 3:18).

IN GALATIANS

In the first chapter of the letter to the Galatians, Paul gives a little history of his background in religion. He says in effect, "Do not speak to me about religion. You could never beat me. I was in that, and I was tops in that. I advanced in religion beyond many of my equals, being 'more exceedingly zealous for the traditions of my fathers' " (v. 14). Traditions always go together with religion. When you are strong for tradition, you are strong for religion, and the outcome is that you will persecute the church. All those who advocate religion will surely be the persecutors of the church. The Apostle Paul said this himself, once in Galatians 1 and again in Philippians 3. "As touching zeal," Paul said, "persecuting the church" (Phil. 3:6). In other words, "When I was in religion, I persecuted the church."

If you are a real Christian, you are a member of the Body of Christ. But be careful; even as a member of the Body of Christ, if you are religious, you will spontaneously persecute the church. I know what I am saying. I have seen many good Christians, many members of the Body of Christ, who have done much damage to the church. They were simply for religion; they were simply religious. These people justify their actions by pointing out certain verses in the Scriptures. They are not the unbelievers, they are not the Jews, they are the real Christians who are so religious. They care for the Christian religion; they do not care for the church life. Some would not damage the church openly, but they undermine it in a subtle way.

The two outstanding essentials of the church life are: 1) to keep the oneness and 2) to be in the spirit. In fact, all we need for the church life may be summed up in this. The slogan, "In the spirit, on the ground," epitomizes these matters. "On the ground" means to keep the oneness, and "in the spirit" simply means that we must do everything in spirit. The reason for all the criticism and persecution of the church life is simply due to these two matters. People care more for religion than being in the spirit and keeping the oneness.

If we mean business for the church life, we must be all-inclusive. Unless the church is involved in sin, immorality, or idolatry, we must go along with it. Whether the meetings are noisy or silent, whether the saints speak in tongues or do not speak in tongues, whether they pray-read or do not pray-read, we must keep the oneness in the local church. Suppose a brother comes in with bare feet. We cannot chase him away. We cannot say, "Brother, go home and get your shoes; otherwise, you cannot come back." As long as he believes in the Lord Jesus, as long as he loves the Lord Jesus, he is our dear brother. We must love him, not because he has bare feet, but because he has Jesus Christ. If you feel you must speak in tongues, then speak in tongues. If you feel that as a sister you should have your head covered, then cover it. If you prefer not to cover your head, then do not trouble those who do. Would you, or could you be so all-inclusive?

The problem today is this: those who speak in tongues always insist that others should speak in tongues, and those who do not speak in tongues would prohibit all others from doing so. We should not care for religion; we should only care for Christ. If we only care for Christ, nothing will bother us. We will be one with all the brothers and sisters. If we all care for Christ and nothing else, we will always be one; there will be no problem.

We must be here not caring for anything but Christ and the church. We may have all things: we may have pray-reading, we may have speaking in tongues, we may have head covering, we may have bare feet, we may have all other things that are not sinful. Could you say that bare feet are sinful? They are not sinful. You may say that you do not like bare feet, but the Lord may say that He isn't concerned about that. Some may say, "I simply cannot go along with anyone playing the tambourine in a meeting." For my part, I am not for it or against it; I am just neutral. If someone feels that he should play the tambourine in the meeting, let him play it. What is wrong with that? We do not care for all these things—we just care for Christ. It is this that makes us one.

Some may charge us with being too liberal; they may call us "liberal Christians." But be careful: this term "liberal Christian" refers to the modernists who do not believe that the Bible is the divine revelation, nor that Jesus Christ is the Son of God, who accomplished redemption, was resurrected, and ascended to the heavens. They are the liberal ones; we are not. We would die for the Bible. We believe that the Bible is God's divine Word, and we believe that our Lord Jesus is the very God incarnated to be a man, who died on the cross for our sins, and was resurrected physically, spiritually, and literally. We believe furthermore that today He is in the heavens as well as dwelling within us as the life-giving Spirit, and that one day He will return, physically and literally. You cannot call us liberal. We are the most fundamental among the fundamentalists. We believe furthermore that there is one Head and one Body, one Shepherd, one flock, one Christ, one Church, and one local church for one city.

We are not liberal, and neither are we legal. We do not have legality in letters. In all the minor matters of the Scriptures we never press the point in a legal way. We never will compromise, however, on the person and work of Christ. We admit being legal in this matter. We do not care for religion, even a Christian religion; we just care for the living Christ.

Paul tells us in Galatians 1 how much he was involved in religion and how zealously he persecuted the church of God. What is the church? The church is not anything of religion; the church is just the expression of the living Christ. This is exactly why those religionists persecuted the church. The church is Christ in an enlarged way. If you are just for Christ, be ready to suffer persecution, not from the unbelievers, but from the Christians, the religious people.

We have seen how in Acts 10 Peter received a vision and learned that there is no difference today between the Jews and the Gentiles, between the clean creatures and the unclean. It seemed that he learned the lesson well, but look now at his behavior in Galatians 2. When Peter came to Antioch he ate with all the brothers, including the Gentile brothers. But when the Jewish brothers came down from Jerusalem, Peter separated himself from the Gentiles, pretending not to associate with them. Could you imagine that Peter would be such a cowardly person? Peter knew that he should not keep that kind of religion, but he feared the Jewish brothers, and not only he, but also Barnabas. Paul was so bold at that time to stand with Christ versus religion. He resisted Peter to his face. It is so easy to pretend to be religious. You may shout, "Hallelujah, praise the Lord," but when you are in the presence of certain brothers, you will not shout. You will become, not a bold Paul, but a cowardly Peter.

We have seen, however, that even Paul in the latter part of his life was not so bold. In Jerusalem, in that intense atmosphere of religion, Paul was subdued and went along with the religious situation in order to save trouble. Let me tell you, whenever you go along with religion to save trouble, you will have more trouble. We may go along with religion, but the Lord Jesus will never go along with religion. Never try to avoid trouble in following the Lord. The more you boldly face the trouble, the less trouble you will have. If you ever consider being mild and compromising a bit, be sure that you are about to involve yourself in many difficulties. Always beware of acting like Peter and Barnabas in Galatians 2 and the Apostle Paul in Acts 21. Today is a day of confusion. Today is also a day of a battle being waged between Christ and religion.

Paul tells us in his letter to the Galatians that if we attempt to keep religion, we will lose Christ and Christ will become of no effect to us. "Behold, I Paul say unto you, that, if ye receive circumcision, Christ will profit you nothing. Ye are severed from Christ, ye who would be justified by the law; ye are fallen away from grace" (Gal. 5:2, 4). If you keep religion, you will lose Christ; and if you keep Christ, you will certainly lose religion. Christ is versus religion; Christ never goes along with religion.

Then Paul tells us in Galatians 6 that it is not a matter of circumcision or uncircumcision, it is not a matter of being a Jew or a Greek; it is a matter of being a new creature in Christ (6:15). He says, "If we live by the Spirit, by the Spirit let us also walk" (5:25). This is all: we just need to walk in the Spirit; we just need to be a new creature, without anything religious.

IN EPHESIANS

Let us look now at the passage in Ephesians 4: "That we may be no longer children, tossed to and fro and carried about with every wind of doctrine, by the sleight of men, in craftiness, after the wiles of error; but holding the reality in love, may grow up in all things into Him, who is the head, even Christ" (vv. 14, 15 Gk.). I do not know whether you have seen something here which is still of religion. Of course, the word "religion" is not mentioned, but something of religion definitely is mentioned. Paul said that we should no longer be carried about with "every wind of doctrine." Notice that it does not say "heresy," but "doctrine." "Every doctrine" is undoubtedly something of religion. Contrasted with the wind of doctrine in this passage are the words "holding the reality." The reality is Christ. We must hold the reality in love that we may grow into Christ. So we see here that Christ is versus doctrine, or in other words, Christ is versus religion.

In Ephesians 4 we read that all the prophets, apostles, evangelists, shepherds, and teachers were given by the Head to the Body for the perfecting of the saints. The perfecting of the saints means making the saints to grow. We feed the saints that they may grow and thus participate in the work of the ministry. The end result is that the saints build up the Body of Christ. The building up of the church is not done directly by the apostles, prophets, evangelists, shepherds or teachers, but by the saints, "until we all arrive at the unity of the faith and of the knowledge of the Son of God, unto a full grown man, unto the measure of the stature of the fulness of Christ" (v. 13 Gk.). The saints are being perfected, and we are all going on until we arrive at three things: 1) The unity of the faith and of the knowledge of the Son of God. The unity here is of two things—the faith and the knowledge of the Son of God. 2) A full grown man. While we are going on, we are growing until we all arrive at a full grown man. 3) The measure of the fulness of Christ. If we refer to chapter 1, verse 23, we see that the fulness of Christ is just the Body. The measure of the fulness of Christ is the measure of the Body.

Notice clearly at this point that verse 13 does not say, "Until we all arrive at the unity of the doctrine and the teachings concerning the Son of God." It does not mean that. It says, "Until we all arrive at the unity of the faith and of the knowledge [the knowing] of the Son of God." If we care overmuch for the doctrine, we are indeed religious. We must see clearly the difference between faith and doctrine. Our Christian faith is entirely different from Christian doctrine. Simply stated it is this: Jesus Christ is the Son of God, who was incarnated as a man, who died on the cross for our sins, who was resurrected bodily from the dead, who ascended to the heavens, who now indwells our spirit, and is coming back soon. This is our faith, and we are all one in this. Besides this faith, however, there are many doctrines. Concerning even one matter, the second coming of the Lord Jesus, there are numerous teachings. Some say that Jesus will return after the tribulation; others insist that He will come before the tribulation; and still others say that He will return in the midst of the tribulation. We all believe that Jesus will come again—this is our faith. Every genuine Christian believes this, and there is no problem as far as that simple fact is concerned. But the matter of exactly when He will return divides Christians. We must see that all these doctrines or teachings concerning the exact time of the Lord's return have nothing to do with our faith. Our faith is what saves us—if we do not have the faith, we can never be saved. Whether we believe in the pre-tribulation, post-tribulation, or mid-tribulation return of the Lord, it has nothing whatever to do with our salvation. It is not holding any specific doctrine concerning the Lord's return that saves us. All we need to do is keep the faith, not the doctrines.

Suppose that three brothers, born of the same parents, attend a Gospel meeting and all are saved. That means they have all received the same faith. Now suppose that after being saved one goes to a Presbyterian seminary, another to a Methodist college, and the third to a Baptist university. After a year's time they will all collect and adhere to many diverse doctrines, and when they come together, they will undoubtedly debate and argue with one another. You see, immediately after they were saved, they had the faith, they could be one. But in addition to the faith, they proceeded to gather all kinds of doctrines. They began with something good, but they started to collect "junk"—I would use such a strong word. And then they began to love the junk. We may use another word and say that they began to gather "toys." The many doctrines which divide so many of the Lord's children today are simply toys.

Now suppose that these three brothers who have collected their "toys" are confronted by a brother who really knows life, a brother who knows how to make the saints grow. Suppose that this brother comes to them, never speaking about doctrines, but helping them to grow. He teaches them to call on the name of the Lord by saying, "O Lord, Amen, Hallelujah!" All the doctrines and doctrinal differences will spontaneously be dropped and disappear. You see, while we are being fed with something of Christ, we are growing spontaneously and cannot be divided over doctrine.

The younger we are, the more toys to which we hold. I am a grandfather—I do not have one toy. But all my grandchildren have many toys. When we grow up, the toys automatically fall away. Paul was so concerned "that we may be no longer children, tossed to and fro and carried about with every wind of doctrine." The children are those who are carried about by the doctrines; they are carried away from Christ the Head and the church the Body. When all the doctrines are gone, when all the "toys" have been dropped, we are brought back to Christ and the church.

We have all been distracted and carried away from Christ and the church by many kinds of doctrines. Notice: they are doctrines, not heresies. They may be sound, scriptural, and fundamental, but they are carrying people away from Christ and the church, from the Head and the Body. Hallelujah, it is by the growth in life that we drop all the doctrines and arrive at the unity of the faith. Those three brothers in our example were one in the faith at the time of their salvation, but following that, they were carried away by the various doctrines. Then by the growth of life, praise the Lord, they were brought back to arrive at the unity of the faith and the knowledge of the Son of God.

Have you realized that when you collected the doctrines, you collected all kinds of religion? The doctrines are the religious things. I have just mentioned one category of doctrines—the doctrines concerning the Lord's coming. Consider how many doctrines there are concerning baptism. Some believe in being immersed once, others believe in being immersed three times; some believe in being immersed forwards, others backwards; some in natural water, others in flowing water. There are all kinds of teachings concerning baptism. And there are many other categories of doctrines which we have not yet covered.

Are we here for all these things? May the Lord have mercy upon us. We must be here for Christ and the church. This will make us one. It is thus that "all the body fitly framed and knit together through every joint of supply, according to the working in due measure of each several part, maketh growth of the body unto the building up of itself in love" (v. 16). We must drop all the doctrines, give up all the religion, and only hold the reality, which is Christ and the church, His expression. Then we will be one in the unique faith, the saving faith.

IN PHILIPPIANS

In his letter to the Philippians Paul elaborates more on his religious background. He had high attainments in religion; yet what things were gain to him in religion, those he counted loss for Christ. He is even so bold to refer to those religious things as "dung." The Greek word for "dung" means "dog food"; it was the dirty things used for feeding the dogs. To the Apostle Paul, not only all other things, but even all religious things were dog food. So he said in the same chapter, "Beware of the dogs" (3:2). Paul was saying in other words, "Beware of the Judaizers, the religious people."

He also said, "Beware of the concision" (3:2). "Concision" is a contemptuous term for circumcision, referring to what the Judaizers, the religious people practiced—the religious circumcision without reality. Paul was saying, "Do not care for religious things. If you do, you will miss Christ." Paul determined never to miss Christ. He said, "One thing I do, forgetting the things which are behind, and stretching forward to the things which are before, I press on toward the goal unto the prize of the high calling of God in Christ Jesus" (vv. 13, 14). We must realize that if we hold on to our experiences in the past, however good they may be, they will become today's religion to us.

Yesterday's manna can never be today's food; if we keep it, it will stink and breed worms. How pitiful to be continually referring to some experience of ours ten or twenty years ago. We need to experience Christ daily and even hourly in a new way. If we hold on to our past experiences, even those of yesterday, they will become our religion. While you were experiencing those things in the past, you were experiencing them in the presence of the Lord. The Lord, however, is going on today. Why stay there with the good things, the right things, but without His presence? All the good and right things will become your religion. You must press on, forgetting the things which are behind. The fulness of God in Christ is our goal. Paul says, "I press on, if so be that I may lay hold on that for which also I was laid hold on by Christ Jesus" (v. 12). He said in other words, "Christ has gained me for fulness; yet I have not experienced all that fulness yet. I am pressing on to that goal." We do need the Lord's mercy and grace that we may never become stuck in our experiences of the past. We must leave that, abandon that, forget about that, and go on.

IN COLOSSIANS

Going on to Colossians we read, "Take heed lest there shall be anyone that maketh spoil of you..." (2:8). Beware; you will be captured, you will be distracted, you will be frustrated by philosophy, by the traditions of men, by the rudiments of the world, by many things besides Christ. For in Christ "dwelleth all the fulness of the Godhead bodily" (v. 9). Forget about philosophy, forget about the traditions, forget about the rudiments of the world, forget about all things, regardless of how good they are, if they are not Christ. Forget about everything but Christ. Eventually Paul tells us that in the new man, in the church life, there is no Greek or Jew, no barbarian or Scythian. That means that there is no religious or unreligious, no cultured or uncultured. In the church life Christ is all and in all (3:11). In the church we have neither religion nor culture; we only have Christ.

IN HEBREWS

Finally, Paul tells us in Hebrews 7:16 that Christ is a priest, "who hath been made, not after the law of a carnal commandment, but after the power of an endless life." We do not have any regulations or rules, because Christ, the High Priest, ministers the things of God to us, not according to any commandment of letters, but according to the power of an endless life. In the church there is no more religion; there is only the living Christ.

Anything that is traditional, anything that is religious, anything, regardless of how good, "spiritual," scriptural, or fundamental it may be, if it lacks the presence of Christ, we should give it up. Let us abandon all these religious things including our past experiences and care only for the living Christ, the instant Christ, the up-to-date Christ. This is our destiny, and this should also be our destination, our goal. We are pressing forward that we may gain that for which we have been gained of Christ Jesus. We are pressing on that we may experience Christ in a full way.

CHAPTER TWELVE

FIVE STEPS TOWARD A NEW RELIGION

Scripture Reading: Rev. 1:12-18; 2:1-7, 12-21, 24-29; 3:1-6, 14-22; 17:4-5; 18:2, 4; 19:7-8

Now we come to the Book of Revelation, where we also see many things concerning Christ versus religion. We must all realize that the Christ in this book differs distinctly from the Christ in the four Gospels. In the Gospels we see a Christ who is gentle, tender, and mild; but in the Revelation we see a Christ whom we may describe as fierce. In the Gospels, the Apostle could lean upon Christ's breast, but in the Revelation, when John saw Christ, he immediately fell to the earth. The Christ we see in Revelation is One whose eyes are as a flame of fire and whose voice is as the sound of many waters. Why is there this difference? It is because, when we come to the Book of Revelation, the age has changed. Therefore, the aspect and attitude of Christ have also correspondingly changed.

In this Book of Revelation we have religion, but this religion differs from the religion in the Gospels, the Acts, and the Epistles. In all these books, the religion was the old religion, the Jewish religion. But here in the last book of the New Testament, religion takes on a new garb. It is no more the Jewish religion, but the Christian religion, the religion of Christianity. Thus, in the Book of Revelation, Christ is different and religion also is different.

In the seven epistles of the second and third chapters of this book we get a clear view of the new religion, Christianity. The Christian religion has become a real religion, and it has become so by steps. Here in these seven epistles we see five steps toward this new religion. Only two churches among these seven, Smyrna and Philadelphia, have nothing to do with religion. All the rest have very much to do with it, and with each there is a definite step taken towards its formation. There are five churches with five steps which together form the new religion of Christianity.

1. WORK WITHOUT LOVE

The first step towards this new religion of Christianity is an abundance of work for Christ without an intimate and personal love to Him. You may never have considered that an abundance of labor for the Lord could be something that would form a religion. You have probably thought that there is nothing wrong with working hard for the Lord. What is wrong with going to the mission field, teaching the Bible, helping people to know the Lord and be saved? The Lord recognizes all the work, as He did that of the church in Ephesus, but there is a danger. You may labor diligently and accomplish much for the Lord without an intimate and personal love for the Lord Himself.

In the recovery of the church life we must all be on the alert. We must work, we must labor for the Lord, but we must be careful that our work is balanced with intimate and personal love for our dear Lord. Indeed, we need to love Him more than we work for Him. Our love for Him must be more precious, more dear than the work we do for Him. We must not be so concerned for what we accomplish for Christ as much as to what extent we love Him. We need an intimate and personal love for the Lord Jesus, and this love must be the first love, the best love. The word translated "first" in reference to first love (Rev. 2:4) is the same as that translated "best" in reference to the best robe (Luke 15:22). Hence, first love is best love, and this is the love we must maintain continually. We may forget to work for Him, but we must never forget to love Him in the first and best way. He is primarily not our Master, but our Bridegroom. Hallelujah! We must never lose sight of our Lord Jesus as our lovely, precious, and present Bridegroom. To serve Him is secondary; to love Him is primary.

The Lord warned the church in Ephesus, "Remember therefore whence thou art fallen, and repent...or else I come to thee, and will move thy lampstand out of its place" (2:5). The Lord said that if they would not repent and return to their first love, they would lose their light, they would lose the testimony, they would lose the lampstand and be in darkness. In other words, without the first and best love, they would be finished as far as the testimony of the Lord Jesus was concerned. It is quite serious. Abundance of labor for the Lord Jesus does not prove that we have the testimony. It is by loving Him in the first and best way that we have the shining power, the light, the lampstand, and the testimony. The testimony of the shining Jesus is not in the labor for Him, but in the intimate love for His dear self.

The Lord's warning to the church of Ephesus was also coupled with a promise. He said, "To him that overcometh, to him will I give to eat of the tree of life, which is in the Paradise of God" (2:7). These three words always go together—love, light, and life. If we love the Lord intimately, personally, and in the first and best way, we will have the light, and we will have the enjoyment of the life. The Lord Jesus promised that those who overcome to love Him thus would eat of the tree of life. This is not merely a promise for future enjoyment of Himself, but a blessed promise to be fulfilled even today. The proper church life is today's paradise of God—it is here that we may enjoy Christ as the tree of life. Christ is not a collection of teachings—He is the tree of life for our enjoyment. We must learn not to imitate Jesus, not merely to follow Jesus, but to eat Jesus as the tree of life in the church as the paradise of God. Undoubtedly this promise refers mainly to the future, but we may have a real foretaste today. Hallelujah! Many of us can testify that we do have such a foretaste today of Christ as the tree of life in the church life as the paradise of God.

The first step of forming the new religion is that of working so much for the Lord Jesus that we lose the intimate and personal love relationship with Himself. Brothers and sisters, wherever we are, the first thing we must do in the local churches is to love the Lord. The first and greatest impression we must give people in the local churches is not how much we work for Christ, but how much we love Him. Whenever we mention His precious name, we should simply be beside ourselves with love for Him. Let us aim at this, and let us be alert lest we lose it. The second impression we must give people is that in this love of Jesus we love one another. We love Him so intimately, and we love one another. The greatest impression people must receive when they touch the church life is the love in these two aspects—love toward the Lord Jesus and love to one another. Then we will have the lampstand with the shining power and fulness of light to chase away all the darkness. Then we will have the enjoyment of the tree of life and taste it even now in the paradise of God. Hallelujah! If we miss this, we are taking the first step to form a Christian religion.

2. THE DOCTRINE OF BALAAM
AND THE NICOLAITANS

From the church at Ephesus we go on to the church at Pergamos. Here in Pergamos we have the second step. All the steps are continuations: step follows step. If you take the first step, surely you will take the second step. And the second step is composed of two main items: 1) the doctrine of Balaam, 2) the doctrine of the Nicolaitans.

What is the doctrine of Balaam? Balaam was a prophet who worked for money. Thus, his preaching, his teaching, just became a job. Why? It was due to the excess of labor and work. When the church has an overabundance of labor and work, people surely will be hired to perform it. If we love the Lord first and foremost, not caring so much for the work, we need hire no one. The danger in Christianity has been and still is that of paying too much attention to the work without the love. Thus, so many

Christian workers must be hired. In the church, all those who work for the Lord should do so not for money, but out of an intimate and burning love for the Lord Himself. We should serve the Lord because His love is burning within us. We simply love Him; we would like to give every drop of blood for Him. We want to serve Him, but this does not mean a kind of work or labor, but an expression of love. We care nothing for money.

Christianity is involved in altogether too much work. "Let us organize something," they say. "Let us open a mission field; let us send out so many missionaries; let us go to the seminaries and Bible institutes and solicit their graduates." This is just the doctrine of Balaam. Those who are hired, of course, must do the work according to their money. Thus, the service of the Lord is commercialized. This is not only religion, but something worse. If any of us ever conceive of hiring someone in the church to accomplish some task, we are taking the second step in forming a new religion. Whenever we talk about money, we are well on our way. Let us not talk about how many dollars we have, but about how many drops of blood we have. We would not work for money, but for the love of Jesus. We care not for the abundance of money or the lack of money. We serve for the love of Jesus—not with dollars, but with drops of blood. If we serve with a consideration of money we can never do the work of love. If we go out without money, but prepared to shed our blood for the love of Jesus, we will raise up a church with the first and best love, a church which could never afford anything to form a religion.

How is it that Christianity today has become such a dreadful religion? Just because of the matter of money, the doctrine of Balaam.

Inevitably following the doctrine of Balaam is the doctrine of the Nicolaitans. What is this? The word "Nicolaitan" comes from two words in Greek, niko and laos. The word niko means to conquer or subdue, while laos means people. Put together, these two words mean to subdue the people, or in other words, the clergy-laity system. Because the service of the Lord has been commercialized, the clergy-laity system spontaneously appears. This system annuls the function of so many members and kills the Body of Christ. It is a great evil. It has been developed to such an extent in some places that if any of the laity should pray, he would certainly be condemned. This is religion at its worst. Nothing offends the Lord so much as the clergy-laity system.

I have full assurance in my spirit to encourage all the Lord's children to pray and even to shout in the meetings. I do believe that this is the Lord's reaction today. The Lord Jesus is reacting today against religion and culture. He is reacting to the uttermost. We all must hate the doctrine of Balaam and the doctrine of the Nicolaitans.

In the church at Ephesus the practice of the Nicolaitans appeared only as a kind of deed—that was the start. But eventually, in the church at Pergamos, it was developed from a deed into a doctrine. When a deed has been developed into a doctrine, it means that the practice has been commonly justified. The people not only practice it, but hold it as a teaching. What a grievous situation! Today we must put, this detestable practice and teaching of the clergy-laity system under our feet. We must not only cast out the teaching, but chase away every Nicolaitan deed. If you come to the meeting and just sit there waiting for others to function, you are still under the influence of the Nicolaitans. You must be delivered, you must escape, you must break through, even if you have to shout. Today in the local church there must be neither "nico-," nor "-laitans," neither clergy nor laymen. All the brothers and sisters must be functioning, praying, testifying, shouting and praising brothers and sisters. Do not think that to shout in a meeting is a small thing. I tell you, this is the reaction of the Lord. Down with the Nicolaitans and up with Christ! The age has changed. The Lord will tolerate no longer the Nicolaitan, clergy-laity system. If you come to the meeting as a layman, waiting for others to function, you put the Lord Jesus to an open shame.

You may say that for anyone to shout, "Jesus is Lord" or "O Lord Jesus" in the meetings is extremely wild. But, I tell you, when the Lord has reacted throughout history, He has always done it in a "wild," or fierce way. We have seen how John the Baptist acted. The Lord Jesus was ushered in, not in a mild way, but in a "wild" way. Now the Lord Jesus in the Book of Revelation is such a fierce Christ. He is fierce against religion, against unreality, against anything that would distract His people from Himself.

If we are much involved in laboring for the Lord without an adequate personal love for Him, we will surely take the way of Balaam and eventually fall into the doctrine of the Nicolaitans.

3. THE TEACHING OF JEZEBEL

When we come to the church at Thyatira we meet an even worse situation. Following the second step, you will surely have the third. Thus, in Thyatira we see a woman called Jezebel, a woman who has gathered many teachings and calls herself a prophetess. Thus far we have seen the doctrine of Balaam, the doctrine of the Nicolaitans, and now the teaching of Jezebel. This is why we say that we must drop the teachings. Thyatira, according to church history, typifies the Roman Catholic Church, and that false church is called by the Spirit here that evil woman Jezebel. It was she who brought so many pagan teachings and practices into the church and mixed them with the teachings concerning Christ. The result then was idol worship and fornication.

There are three abominations in the eyes of the Lord—idol worship, fornication, and division. Idol worship is an insult to the person of God; fornication is a damage to humanity; and division is a mutilation of the Body of Christ. God cares for Himself, God cares for humanity, and God cares for the Body of Christ. God would never tolerate any idols, any fornication, or any division. Here in the church at Thyatira, the woman Jezebel brought in her evil doctrine and caused much idol worship and fornication. God's divine being was insulted, and the proper humanity was damaged. This is the Roman Catholic religion. It is dreadful to the extreme.

This woman by the name of Jezebel, after being fully developed, becomes the great Babylon. In chapter 2 of Revelation her name is Jezebel, and in chapter 17 her name is Babylon the Great. She is also called the great harlot and the mother of the harlots of the earth. This is the ultimate development of the Christian religion. Step by step was taken; one step led to another. The first step was a superabundance of labor; the second step was the doctrine of Balaam and the doctrine of the Nicolaitans; then the third step opened the door widely to paganism and led directly to Babylon. Babylon is the consummation of Christian religion. How desperate we must be to avoid anything religious!

Do not say that there is nothing wrong with doing missionary work, with organizing a mission and spreading the Gospel for the furtherance of the kingdom. You must be careful. That might be the first step towards the forming of a religion. If you take the first step, you will take the second and then eventually the third until you topple headlong into Babylon.

Now we are in the age of the Lord's recovery. My burden concerning the matter of Christ versus religion is very heavy. I fear that perhaps ten or fifteen years from now history will be repeated. We may soon be taking the first step in an overabundance of work and labor, losing our personal and intimate love for the Lord Jesus in the first and best way. Then we will be on our way to form some kind of religion. We will soon be taking all the doctrines and going the full course in religion. May the Lord be merciful to us. Since we are in the Lord's recovery, we must be clear: we must have nothing to do with the first step, the second or the third step; we must be on the alert not to have anything religious.

4. RIGHT BUT DEAD

In the history of the Lord's recovery, the Lord moved on from Thyatira to Sardis. Sardis was a partial recovery from Thyatira. But according to the Word of the Lord it was only a short time after Sardis appeared that she became a kind of dead religion. What was wrong with Sardis? There was not much wrong; the only problem was that she was dead. The Lord said to her, "Thou hast a name that thou livest, and art dead," and, "Strengthen the things...that are ready to die." In nearly everything, Sardis was in a state of deadness. From church history we see how the church through Martin Luther experienced a certain amount of recovery, but everything soon became dead. To have anything right in a dead way is a kind of religion. If we are sound, fundamental, and scriptural, but dead, we have simply fallen into a religion. If you speak about justification by faith, it is good and right, but if you speak in a dead way, that also is a religion.

I have met a good number of so-called Lutheran believers. The Lutheran Church, we know, stands strongly for Luther's teaching concerning justification by faith, and these followers spoke much with me regarding this matter. They were one hundred percent right, but only in doctrine. They could speak much about justification by faith, but I eventually discovered that they were not justified. They were absolutely correct doctrinally speaking, but they had no experience of what they spoke. This is just a kind of religion. Religious people hold certain religious teachings without any life.

Take this principle and check with various groups in Christianity today. You will find that with nearly all of them the principle is the same—they hold the teachings, but there is no life. Brothers and sisters, I fear that if we are not on the alert, we may hold the right teachings concerning Christ as the life-giving Spirit and yet not have the experience. We may even have the correct teachings concerning such a matter as this, but without the life itself. This also is a religion. Everything we teach, everything we minister, everything we stand for, must be full of life; otherwise, we are perpetuating the history of Sardis. What is the religion of Sardis? It is to hold something so right, so fundamental, and so scriptural, yet without life. Even the matter of the church life and the church ground can be held merely as a right doctrine, stripped of life and impact. Anything that is scriptural and even spiritual, yet without life, becomes religion. The Lord cannot tolerate those who are "deadly right." This is the fourth step.

5. RICH ONLY IN DOCTRINE

In the history of the Lord's move, following the recovery five hundred years ago through Martin Luther, another step was taken by the Lord about one hundred and forty years ago through the so-called Brethren. At the beginning, that was truly the church at Philadelphia, but it did not last long They soon degraded into Laodicea. Philadelphia is an improvement upon Sardis, but Laodicea is a degradation from Philadelphia. What is the problem with Laodicea? It is that Laodicea has everything; they are indeed rich yet, in the same principle as Sardis, just in doctrine. They thought they had everything, they thought they had need of nothing, but the Lord Jesus said that they were neither cold nor hot.

There is a danger in the church life that we too may one day become lukewarm, neither cold nor hot. We may say that we are rich, but we will be rich in doctrine, not in experience. We will be rich, but dead. The Lord Jesus told Laodicea to buy gold that they may be rich and eyesalve that their eyes may be opened. We must be on the alert lest we too have many so-called riches, riches concerning life, concerning the Spirit, concerning the church, yet just in doctrine. We may think that we are so rich, we may think that we know, but we do not see. We may have the knowledge, but not the light. We may have the doctrine, but not the gold. We may not be cold, but neither are we hot; so the Lord will spit us out of His mouth.

Now listen to the promises of the Lord. To the church at Ephesus: "To him that overcometh, to him will I give to eat of the tree of life" (2:7). To the church at Pergamos: "To him that overcometh, to him will I give of the hidden manna..." (2:17). To the church at Laodicea: "If any man hear my voice and open the door, I will come in to him, and will sup with him, and he with me" (3:20). The Lord promised that if we are on the alert to avoid all kinds of religion, we will be kept continually in the enjoyment of the Lord, we will be given to eat of Him as the tree of life, as the hidden manna, and we will sup with Him and He with us.

In the seven epistles of these two chapters of Revelation we see that something of religion has been mixed with something of the Lord. Throughout the centuries up to this present time, the Lord has been doing a separating work to divide all that is of Him from anything religious. All the religious things will be gathered together and consummated to the full in the great Babylon of chapters 17 and 18. Babylon the Great is the consummate development of religion. It is the place to which all the steps towards religion in these epistles lead. On the other hand, the consummate development of all the Lord's separating work throughout the centuries is the Bride, the New Jerusalem. The Lord's separating work for His Bride today is in the local church. The local church is the ultimate part of this separating work to prepare the Bride. Thus, throughout the centuries we see that there has been a move in the history of the church towards mixture. The end of that is Babylon. But throughout the centuries there has also been a divine, separating work in progress. In the last part of this the twentieth century, the Lord is recovering the local churches as a full separation from the great Babylon. Eventually this will result in the final issue of the Lord's separating work, the Bride. Hallelujah! Following Revelation 17 and 18, we come to chapter 19, where the Bride has made herself ready. In chapter 18 we hear the Lord's call, "Come forth, my people, out of her, that ye have no fellowship with her sins" (v. 4). And in chapter 19 we have the word, "The marriage of the Lamb is come, and His wife hath made herself ready" (v. 7). Praise the Lord that we may be in the local church life today, fully separated from anything religious, and thus prepared as the Bride of the Lamb.

In all these chapters we have been seeing Christ versus religion. The ultimate issue of Christ will be the Bride, and the consummate development of religion will be Babylon. Thus, Christ versus religion will eventually be the Bride versus Babylon. It is not a small matter to be separated from everything religious and to be in the local churches as a preparation for the Bride. Hallelujah!

CHAPTER THIRTEEN

THE AGE OF THE BOOK OF REVELATION

Scripture Reading: Rev. 2:1, 7, 8, 11, 12, 17, 18, 29; 3:1a, 6, 7, 13, 14, 22; 14:13b; 22:17a; 5:6; 1:10; 19:10b; 22:6b

NO QUOTATIONS

The age of the Book of Revelation is the age of the seven Spirits, and this is the day in which we are living. Hallelujah for the last book of the Bible, the Book of Revelation! It is entirely different from all the other books. In Matthew there are a number of quotations from the Old Testament. In John, the Acts, Romans, Hebrews, and other books there are also many quotations. But here in the Book of Revelation, a book of twenty-two chapters, we cannot find one Old Testament quotation. It is absolutely a new book; nothing in it is quoted from the old books. In this book there are no quotations from the entire Bible—nothing at all of the old way. Then what is here? The seven Spirits! There is a Lamb with seven eyes, which are the seven Spirits of God. This is all. We only see the Lamb, the Redeemer, with the intensified Spirit. Nothing is of the old source. All the utterances in this book are made by the sevenfold Spirit and are new and fresh. There is nothing religious, nothing old, nothing dead; everything is spoken by the living Spirit in a new and living way.

NO HUMAN SPEAKING

Furthermore, we never read in this book of any human utterances! We always read that it is the Spirit who is speaking. "Yea, saith the Spirit" (14:13). "He that hath

an ear, let him hear what the Spirit saith to the churches"
(2:7, etc.). Seven times in chapters 2 and 3 we read that
it is the Spirit who is speaking to the churches. The
messages here are quite unlike those of the Old Testament
prophets who prophesied, "Yea, my people, thus saith the
Lord..." The utterances here are also unlike those in the
Epistles. The Epistles say, "This I [Paul] say" (I Cor.
7:6), or "I [Peter] exhort" (I Pet. 5:1), etc. Here in the Book of
Revelation it never says, "Thus saith the Lord," or "This
I say," etc. It says rather, "The Spirit saith, the Spirit
saith, the Spirit saith." Have you noticed this same
sentence with the same wording repeated seven times:
"He that hath an ear, let him hear what the Spirit saith
to the churches"? Why is this sentence repeated seven
times? Because of the seven-fold Spirit. Eventually the
entire book is concluded in this way: "And the Spirit and
the bride say..." (22:17). We read firstly in this book that
the Spirit is speaking to the churches. Then eventually
the Spirit and the Bride become one—they speak together.
The Spirit and the church in this verse are a compound
subject. The two have been compounded; the two have
become one. Hallelujah! The church is one with the seven
Spirits, and the seven Spirits have been fully wrought
into the church. This is God's goal! This is the ultimate
consummation of His eternal purpose.

NO DOCTRINES, NO GIFTS, NO GIFTED PERSONS

Neither can we find in the Book of Revelation any
doctrines, gifts, or even any gifted persons. There are no
apostles, no prophets, no evangelists, no shepherds or
pastors here; neither are there any elders or deacons.
What we see here are the angels in the local churches.
The angels are the stars, and the stars are related to the
seven Spirits just as the seven churches are also related
to the seven Spirits. The seven Spirits are for the seven
churches, and the seven Spirits are also for the seven
stars.

What is the meaning of all this? We must realize that
by the time of the Book of Revelation the age has been

fully changed from religion to the Spirit. Why in this book are there no more doctrines, gifts, gifted persons, elders or deacons? Because all these things have been so extensively utilized by the subtle enemy to form a religion. Thus, at this point in the Scriptures and in the Lord's recovery, the Spirit does not mention all these things. Could anyone form a religion of the seven Spirits? I tell you, the seven Spirits will wipe out all religious elements.

In a certain place recently two young people were much helped by the fellowship of other young people in the meetings of the local church. The following day these two, a boy and a girl, stood together with their mother in the meeting to declare, "Down with Satan!" The father of those two youngsters was there and was greatly offended. He came to the front and told the whole congregation how grieved he was with such an exclamation, "Down with Satan!" He said, "If Satan were here, you would all be terrified." Upon this all the brothers and sisters in the meeting began to shout, "Down with Satan! Down with Satan!" The father then called the mother and, motioning for the children to follow, stalked out of the meeting. Later I learned that these parents were godly members of a certain group of Christians famous for knowing the doctrines of the Bible. But consider: what is wrong with Christians saying, "Down with Satan"? On the contrary, I would say that it is marvelous. Yet godly members of a certain group with a name for knowing the doctrines of the Bible were offended. This is religion.

Brothers and sisters, I fear that if you were living in the days of John the Baptist and were accustomed to offering sacrifices in the temple in a well-ordered way, you would be utterly shocked at John the Baptist. If you went to the wilderness and saw John wearing the camel's hair and eating the locusts and wild honey, you would say, "What is this? Is this a man or an animal? Could such a person be God's prophet? Why doesn't he speak in the temple?" But who are you? Are you the Lord? I am not rebuking you. What I am saying is that we must all realize we have been trapped by religion, even by Christianity. Christianity is a subtle snare—it has ensnared all Christians. Let me say a word to you—I don't mean others, I mean you. You still have at least a few drops of religion in your blood.

Have you realized by reading the record of the Lord's birth in the four Gospels that it was absolutely different from the expectation of those who held the Old Testament in their hands? All the religious people were well aware of the prophecies concerning the birth of Christ and were expecting the Messiah to be born. But eventually, when He was born, it was utterly contrary to their expectation. Those who held the Bible paid no attention whatever to the actual event. And when the Lord Jesus came forth at the age of thirty for His ministry, none of the religious ones recognized Him. Do you not believe that the same situation will prevail at the Lord's second coming? So many New Testament saints hold the Bible in their hands today, knowing and proclaiming the second coming of the Lord. Eventually, when the Lord Jesus comes, He will come utterly contrary to their expectation. They will be blinded by religion.

We have been indoctrinated with so many religious concepts—we do not know how many. They have been indoctrinated into our nature, into our life, into our blood. It seems easier for the young people to rid themselves of religious blood, but this is just the outward appearance. Don't think that because you are released and shout that you are free from religion. The religious concept is not in your outward activity, but in your inward disposition. It is in your blood, your nature. For the older ones, breaking the ties and getting the religion out of the blood is even more difficult. We simply do not know how many religious concepts have been wrought into our being.

NO POSITIONS, NO TITLES

Anything without the presence of Christ is just a religion to us. The spiritual experiences of yesterday

applied to today's situation is just a religion. When we
come to the Book of Revelation, suddenly everything is
changed. There are even no more positions, no more titles.
In the local churches of the Epistles, there are firstly the
elders or bishops, and then the deacons and so forth. There
are the titles—apostles, prophets, evangelists, and shepherds and teachers. But when we come to the Book of
Revelation, all these are gone. Paul wrote to the churches
as "an apostle of Christ Jesus" (Eph. 1:1), but John in the
Revelation speaks of himself as "your brother" (1: 9). By
the time John wrote the Book of Revelation, he was close
to one hundred years of age. He was really qualified and
experienced as an apostle; he did have the position. At
the time he wrote Revelation, he was the last of the
original twelve apostles left on the earth, but he never
referred to himself as such in this book. Have you seen
this? "I John, your brother," he said. That is all. That was
the position, that was the qualification he assumed in
this book. Why? Because in the Lord's economy in this
book and in this age all these things—position, title,
qualification—are over.

Today, in the age of the spirit, there is no position, no
title, and no qualification. There is only one thing—the
sevenfold Spirit. There are no elders; there are only stars.
You may presume to be a proper elder, but you can never
presume to be a star. If you are a star, you must shine.
It is a shame today to claim the position of being an elder.
It is a shame today to claim any position because of your
many years of experience. It matters not how long you
have been in the work of the Lord, but it matters very
much whether you are shining or not. Are you shining?
Are you living? Are you burning? The Lord today in the
age of the Spirit does not care for anything—your
experiences, your position, or your qualifications—but for
the seven burning Spirits. Have you been burned by the
seven Spirits? And are you burning in the sevenfold Spirit?

Today is not the day of the Epistles; today is the day
of the Revelation. Today is not the day of the elders; today

is the day of the shining stars. Oh, the deadness, oh, the deadness of claiming the position of an elder! That is a religion, and it will eventually become a part of the great Babylon. The position which you claim will never be in the New Jerusalem. Those who claim positions are as dead as doornails. There is no flow among them. There is nothing living, nothing burning, nothing shining. To claim a position, to claim a certain title, is nothing but a kind of religion. That is not life, that is not Christ—that is religion.

After reading so much concerning Christ versus religion, you may still not know what religion is. You may be criticizing other brothers, criticizing the responsible ones, criticizing the co-workers. What is this? This too is religion. "Oh, the Lord be merciful to us! O Lord Jesus! O Lord Jesus! How much we need Your rescue, Lord! We need Your deliverance! Deliver us from the positions, deliver us from the titles, deliver us from the qualifications, and deliver us from the criticisms." All of these things belong to Babylon the Great; they will never be in the New Jerusalem. In Babylon there are the pope, the cardinals, the bishops, etc.—many positions, many titles. But in the churches there are no positions, no titles, no qualifications. There is just the sevenfold Spirit with the shining stars.

You may claim that you are in the local church. But is that really the lampstand in your city? Is it shining? Oh, the Lord be merciful to us. Do not ask, "Are we not the house of God? Are we not the local church?" What about the shining? Where is the lampstand? Is there anything shining in the darkness of your city, in the night of this age?

HOW TO READ REVELATION

We must all see the character of today's age. It is no more the age of religion. It is no more the age of mere quotations. It is no more the age of mere teachings or doctrines. It is no more the age of the gifts or the gifted persons. It is no more the age of the so-called elders and deacons. This is the age of the Book of Revelation. This is the age of the seven Spirits for the seven churches with the seven stars. In this book the Lord Jesus declares that He is the living One (1:18). What good is it to hold the sound and scriptural doctrines as long as you are dead? Oh, the doctrines! Oh, the teachings! Oh, the gifts! Oh, the dissension! Oh, the deadness! How much we need to give up our concepts and our dissenting thoughts! How much we need to come to the Book of Revelation and to the age of this book! The Book of Revelation is the stepping stone to the New Jerusalem. If we have never been in the reality of the Book of Revelation, we can never be in the New Jerusalem. Let us drop all the oldness and get into it. Let us just take one word—Amen—and mingle it with the words of this book. The seven churches—Amen! The seven Spirits—Amen! Seven angels—Amen! Seven stars—Amen! One city, one church—Amen! One church, one city—Amen! The church at Ephesus—Amen! The church at Smyrna—Amen! The church at Pergamos— Amen! Even if I don't understand, I still must say Amen. Even if I don't agree, I still must say Amen. I am not the Lord—He is the Lord! If we would do this we would be exceedingly blessed; we would be the most favored people on this earth. We would have rest and we would be so very happy. We would not care what people say—we would only care what the seven Spirits say.

I would not suggest that you burn all your books, but I beg you to put all your books aside and come to the last book of the Bible. The last book of the Bible is the last word of the Lord, and the last word of any person is the most important. The last word of the Bible is the Book of Revelation. Let us pray-read every chapter with every verse, every phrase with every word, and say Amen every time. We need not attempt to understand or analyze it. We need only say Amen to every word. I challenge you to try it and see what the result will be. I have full assurance that you will be set on fire by the sevenfold Spirit.

UP-TO-DATE WITH THE LORD

The year is not 1770 nor 1870, but 1970. The Lord is marching on. We thank the Lord for all His previous recoveries throughout the past generations—without them we could never have reached the present age. But we must be up-to-date with the Lord. We should not linger behind in some past age of the Lord's move. Since we are in 1970, we should be in tune with the Lord's move in 1970. May the Lord deliver us from being backward Christians. We need to be brought on and on. This month is different from last month, and today is different from yesterday. We expect that tomorrow the Lord will go on to accomplish something further. Why must we hold on to so many old things?—that is Satan's subtle snare. We all need to be rescued by the present Jesus. What was good for yesterday may be the snare of the enemy to you today.

Let me say a word to the senior brothers and sisters. I am not so young; I know all your problems. Your problems can be summed up in three categories: 1) the doctrines you have learned, 2) the experiences through which you have passed, 3) all the things you have seen in the past. But in the Book of Revelation, I say again, there are no doctrines, there are no experiences, and there is nothing of the past. We all need to have a new start. The Apostle John in this book is absolutely new, absolutely different from the John in the Gospel and in the three Epistles. Listen to his tone in the Revelation. Why is there such a change? Because he was in the spirit and heard the voice; because he turned himself and saw something new. Oh, how we need to overcome the old doctrines, the old experiences, and all the things we have seen in the past! We need to overcome and we need to come over. Don't say that you sympathize with the young people because they are young and must be so active. There is no need for you to sympathize with them. Sympathize with yourself! No one is so pitiful as you. Ask the Lord to have mercy on you.

The seven Spirits of God are sent forth into all the earth (5:6). The seven Spirits today are just like the air throughout the entire earth. They are not only in Los Angeles—they are everywhere. Never say that such an intensified Spirit is only good for Los Angeles. You may say that Los Angeles is Los Angeles and every church must have its own separate and distinct expression. But what is your expression? I fear that it may be the expression of deadness, the expression of your dissenting thought. Christianity is just the expression of dead religion, the expression of so many divisive things. The sevenfold intensified Spirit is sent forth into all the earth.

THE SPIRIT OF PROPHECY

Never think that the Book of Revelation is merely a book of prophecy. We have read Revelation 19:10 saying that "the testimony of Jesus is the spirit of prophecy." I agree that Revelation is a book of prophecy, but you must not merely care for the prophecy and forget the Spirit. We would rather forget the prophecy and care for the Spirit. When you come to this book, don't try to analyze and understand it. Just say Amen from your spirit to every word; then you will be endued with the spirit of prophecy. To be concerned with the prophecies is one thing; to care for the spirit of the prophecies is another.

THE GOD OF OUR SPIRITS

The last chapter of this book says that the Lord is "the God of the spirits of the prophets" (22:6). God is the God of our spirits; He is not the God of our mind; He is not the God of our outward activities. Never get into your mind, never get into the teachings, never get into the doctrines. You can never meet God in all those realms—He is not there. God is in your spirit. God is the God of your spirit. You must be in your spirit to be with God and touch God. Today I am at a certain address in Los Angeles. If you go to San Francisco, you will miss me. If you go to any other street in Los Angeles, you will miss me. If you stand outside my house on the street corner, you will miss me. You must come to the door and enter my dwelling to be where I am. God is the God of the spirits of the prophets. We all need to turn to our spirit. This is why the Apostle John was in spirit.

Today is the age of the Book of Revelation. In this age the sevenfold, intensified Spirit of God is versus religion. Let us look to the Lord desperately that we all may be fully taken out of religion and religion fully taken out of us. May we only be the seven shining stars in the seven burning lampstands with the sevenfold, intensified Spirit. O Lord! Amen!

CHAPTER FOURTEEN

THE LEAVEN AND THE HARLOT

Scripture Reading: Matt. 13:33, 45, 46; Rev. 17:3-5; 19:7, 8;
21:10, 11, 18, 19a; 22:1; 21:6; 22:17

LEAVEN HID IN THE MEAL

In the New Testament, from the first book to the last,
there are always two main things revealed. These two
matters are clearly set before us in Matthew 13. One of
them, on the one side, is the leaven taken by the woman
and hid in the meal. We must see clearly that this leaven
was not merely put into the meal, but "hid" in the meal.
The meal is visible and apparent, but actually a corrupting, filthy, and defiling element is hidden within it. What
is observed by our visible perception is the meal; it is
more difficult to discern that leaven is hidden within it.
You may say, "Look, is this not meal? Is this not good for
food?" Yes, but listen, some thing corrupting, damaging,
filthy, worldly, and sinful, is hidden within it. May the
Lord open our eyes, not just to see apparently, but to see
discernibly that which is hidden. The meal is indeed good
for food; it is the very thing that God is after. No one has
any problem with the meal. But we must see what is
hidden within the meal. It is the leaven. And who put the
leaven into the meal? Of course, not God, neither the
church, but a woman. And who is the woman? The Roman
Catholic Church, the great harlot and mother of all
harlots.

I am greatly concerned that, after speaking so much
concerning religion and Babylon and linking these matters
with the Christianity of today, you may say, "That is too

much. Are there not many good works for the Lord in Christianity? Have there not been many who have gone to the mission fields and helped people know God? Have there not been many ministers who have helped others grow in Christ?" Yes, undoubtedly. But consider this parable spoken by the Lord Jesus. The Lord refers to meal, real meal. But we must see that within this meal, hidden to the natural sense, is a certain element called leaven inserted by an evil woman. In the entire Bible, both in the Old Testament and in the New, leaven is set forth as a corrupting, damaging, evil element. The meal is good; the meal is the thing that God is after. But within this God-blessed substance is something sown which is sinful, devilish and evil. We all must see this. There is no argument.

We must certainly admit that in today's Christianity there are many good works. We can even say the same for the Roman Catholic Church. But within these good works is a subtle element. Oh, the devilish subtlety in this matter! Something of the devil, something of Satan, something of the enemy has been put into the meal in a subtle way. People today only see the meal; they are quite blind to the leaven.

THE PEARL VERSUS THE LEAVENED MEAL

Now we must see the second matter, the other side. In the same chapter, Matthew 13, we see the Lord as a merchant willing to pay any price for a certain article. What is it He is seeking? It is not the meal (which has been leavened). He is seeking a goodly pearl. Can you leaven a pearl? Can you hide something within a pearl? Impossible. A pearl is something solid, something pure.

We all must see these two things, one on one side and one on the other. Have you seen them? Have you seen the leaven in the meal on one side, and the pearl which is so solid and pure on the other? These are two things: the leaven hidden in the meal is one, and the pearl of great price is another. With which are you standing? Are you one with the pearl, or are you one with the meal and the leaven? I do not believe that any among us would want to be so stupid as to take sides with the leavened meal. But in fact, some even of those who are reading this book are taking sides deeply within them with the leavened meal. They are arguing, or at least they are trying to argue, for the defense of this meal. They have not seen the evil nature of the corrupting leaven. Neither have they seen that the entire meal is permeated with the leaven. Opposed to the leavened meal on the other hand is something so solid and incorruptible—the pearl. It could never be damaged by the evil woman or even by her daughters. Where do we stand?

THE GREAT HARLOT

Now we go on from the first book of the New Testament to the last, from the beginning to the end. Here in the Book of Revelation two females are clearly presented. One is that evil woman again. The same woman mentioned in Matthew 13 is now in Revelation 17. The one who took the leaven and hid it in the meal in Matthew 13 is the great harlot, the mother of all harlots, in Revelation 17. She is arrayed with purple and scarlet and decked with gold, precious stones and pearls. Such an evil woman is gilded with all the materials of the New Jerusalem; yet she is filled with abominations. In outward appearance she looks like the New Jerusalem—this is her pretension. But in inward reality she is filled with all blasphemies, abominations, and filthiness. She is gilded with three categories of things—gold, precious stones, and pearls; but she is filled with another three categories of things—blasphemies, abominations, and filthiness.

In Christendom today two groups of things are put together by the enemy. On the one hand there is the gold, the precious stones, and the pearls—these are the things which God is after. But on the other hand, there are the blasphemies, the abominations, and the filthiness—these are the things God detests. Christianity combines these two groups in a dreadful mixture. The subtle thing is this: Christendom has gilded itself with the materials of the New Jerusalem. We must see through the gilding to the inward reality. We need a discerning and transparent vision, not just to judge according to appearance, but to see to the core. Apparently in Christendom there is gold, precious stones, and pearls, but actually there are blasphemies, abominations, and filthiness. These two categories are combined in one person, one woman, one evil female.

What is this? This is the leavened meal. Revelation 17 is the full development of Matthew 13. The consummation of the leavened meal is the great harlot and mother of all harlots. What is the source then of the gold, the precious stones, and the pearls? Undoubtedly, the meal. These are all constituents of the good substance, the meal. You may ask who the precious stones are in the Roman Catholic Church. Madame Guyon was certainly one, and there were many others. What is the source of the blasphemies, abominations, and filthiness? That, of course, is the leaven. We must all see that not only in the Bible, but also today in this universe on this earth, there is such an evil female gilded with all the precious materials of God's holy city, yet filled with all the filthiness of the filthy one, the devil. I say again, such a one, such an evil woman is on this earth today. We all must be on the alert never to be involved with her. We may not be involved with her directly, but it is exceedingly easy to be involved with some of her daughters. Not only is this evil woman present on earth, but also her evil daughters. She has many daughters, some greater and some smaller. The bigger they are, the easier they are to discern; the smaller they are, the more easily you are fooled. You may be quite clear and resolute never to be involved with the Roman Catholic Church. You may also be clear never to join any of the denominations. But be careful: you may easily become involved with one of the little daughters of that great harlot. You may flirt with and eventually marry not the eldest daughter, but the youngest.

THE BRIDE VERSUS THE HARLOT

But on the other side, in Revelation chapters 19 and 21, we have another woman, the Bride, the wife of the Lamb. She is dressed in fine linen, bright and pure. There is nothing mixed about her. In chapter 21, we see that this holy female, the Bride, is the holy city, the New Jerusalem. That city is built up and constituted (not gilded) of gold, precious stones, and pearls. The city proper is pure gold, clear as crystal. There is no mixture, and there is nothing hidden. Apparently and actually, outwardly and inwardly, in any way and in every way, it is gold. The city is pure gold. And the wall is built firstly with jasper, which signifies the appearance of God (Rev. 4:3), and then with all manner of precious stones. As for the gates, every gate is a pearl in itself. How marvelous! This is not a gilded article, but one which has been transformed from center to circumference. This is exactly what it is—it is gold, it is precious stone, and it is pearl. Revelation 17 records the full development of the leavened meal in Matthew 13, and Revelation 21 records the full development of the pearl in Matthew 13.

These are the two signs. Never think that in Babylon there is no gold, precious stone, or pearl. Not only are there many who are saved in the denominations, but there are many precious stones there. But look at the picture: if you have seen the vision, could you take sides with great Babylon? Could you say that since there are so many precious stones in Babylon you should remain there? May the Lord open His Word and open your understanding. May the Lord grant you clear and transparent discernment that you may say, "Regardless of how much gold is there, regardless of how many precious stones and pearls are there, that is still the great Babylon, the great harlot, the mother of all the harlots." Some dear Christians are rather simple and think that as long as other Christians are in Babylon it is all right. You may say it is all right, but the Lord says *NEVER*. We must take sides with that which is solid and pure. Do not be fooled, do not be deceived, do not be cheated. You must see that there are two sides in the Bible, the mixture side and the pure side, the Babylon side and the New Jerusalem side. To continue to say, "Is that not a good work? Are there not many saved ones there?" simply proves that you have never received divine discernment. If you can say that, you have never seen what our Brother John saw.

In Revelation 17 John said in effect, "I was carried away in spirit into the wilderness, where I saw that subtle female, that evil woman. Oh, she is so subtle! She stole the precious materials from the New Jerusalem with which to gild herself and cheat others. She is not for those precious things; she is for the devilish blasphemies, abominations, and filthiness." Brothers and sisters, we all must be carried away from today's Christendom to the wilderness and look back. Look at it from a distance, look at it from God's viewpoint. You will see that there are undoubtedly some saved ones and even some precious stones there. But you will also see that she is filled with the names of blasphemy, abominations and filthiness. You will become clear by being carried away in the spirit to the wilderness.

But John, our brother, was also carried away in the spirit to a great and high mountain, from which he looked down and saw the Holy City, the New Jerusalem, not gilded, but built up with gold, pearls, and precious stones. Which side would you take? Tell me, which side would you take?

THE FLOW OF LIVING WATER

In the great Babylon there is gold, precious stone and pearl, but there is no flow of the living water. In the New Jerusalem, however, in the city which is built of gold, precious stones, and pearls, there is a pure river of water of life flowing out of the throne of the redeeming God. The call is sent out, "Come!" Come where? Come to the great Babylon? You cannot get the water there. "He that is athirst, let him come: he that will, let him take the water of life freely" (22:17). You must come out of Babylon, you must come to the New Jerusalem to drink. If you are in a place where you sense there is no river, no flowing, but on the contrary a dry and barren land, you must be clear that you are either in the great harlot or in one of her little daughters. The first sign that you have entered a genuine local church is that you meet something flowing, something watering, something which quenches your thirst. You may discern the situation by seeing whether or not there is a flowing river. You may see the gold, the precious stones, and the pearls in Babylon, but you can never find the flow of the living water there. There is nothing there to quench your thirsty spirit. Which is Babylon and which is the local church? Find where the river flows—that is the local church. "And He said unto me...I will give unto him that is athirst of the fountain of the water of life freely" (21:6). This is the sign of the local churches.

CHRIST AS EVERYTHING

Eventually and ultimately Christ will be manifested and expressed in the New Jerusalem as everything for eternity. He is "the Alpha and the Omega, the first and the last, the beginning and the end" (Rev. 22:13). He is everything! As the center of the Holy City, He is the Lamb on the throne with God within Him as His content (Rev. 22:1). As the expression of God, He is the Lamp shining forth. with the glory of God, who is the light within Him (Rev. 21:23—"light" in Greek is "lamp"). As the presence of God, He is the temple within the Holy City (Rev. 21:22), in which the saints as the priests worship and serve God. As the life supply to the entire city, He is the tree of life in the flow of the river of water of life (Rev. 22:2). As the ultimate manifestation of the fulness of the Godhead, He is the reality of every part of the Holy City. He will be magnified there with all His riches to the uttermost as everything in the ultimate manifestation of God's economy. There will be no more religion, no more doctrine, no more teaching, no more regulations, forms and rituals. There will be no more "-isms"—no more heathenism, no more paganism, no more Catholicism, no more Protestantism, no more fundamentalism, no more Pentecostalism, no more denominationalism, and no more sectarianism. Christ will be everything. All religious things will be past; everything will be purely Christ. There will be no ground for anything religious—Christ will have all the ground. Everywhere and everything will be Christ. Christ will be the center and the circumference. Christ will be the inward content and the outward expression. Christ will be all in all! Hallelujah! May Christ be such in every local church today! Amen!

Not the law of letters,
　　But the Christ of life
God desires to give us,
　　Saving us from strife;
It is not some doctrine,
　　But 'tis Christ Himself
Who alone releases
　　From our sinful self.

Any kind of teaching,
　　Any kind of form,
Cannot quicken spirits
　　Or our souls transform;
It is Christ in Spirit
　　Gives us life divine,
Thus through us to live the
　　Life of God's design.

Not philosophy nor
　　Any element
Can to Christ conform us
　　As His complement;
But 'tis Christ Himself who
　　All our nature takes
And in resurrection
　　Us His members makes.

Not religion, even
　　Christianity,
Can fulfill God's purpose
　　Or economy;
But 'tis Christ within us
　　As our all in all
Satisfies God's wishes,
　　And His plan withal.

All the gifts we're given
　　By the Lord in grace,
All the different functions
　　Cannot Christ replace.

Only Christ Himself must
  Be our all in all!
Only Christ Himself in
  All things, great or small!

(Hymn #541 in *Hymns*)

ABOUT THE AUTHOR

Witness Lee was born in 1905 in northern China and raised in a Christian family. At age 19 he was fully captured for Christ and immediately consecrated himself to preach the gospel for the rest of his life. Early in his service, he met Watchman Nee, a renowned preacher, teacher, and writer. Witness Lee labored together with Watchman Nee under his direction. In 1934 Watchman Nee entrusted Witness Lee with the responsibility for his publication operation, called the Shanghai Gospel Bookroom.

. Prior to the Communist takeover in 1949, Witness Lee was sent by Watchman Nee and his other co-workers to Taiwan to ensure that the things delivered to them by the Lord would not be lost. Watchman Nee instructed Witness Lee to continue the former's publishing operation abroad as the Taiwan Gospel Bookroom, which has been publicly recognized as the publisher of Watchman Nee's works outside China. Witness Lee's work in Taiwan manifested the Lord's abundant blessing. From a mere 350 believers, newly fled from the mainland, the churches in Taiwan grew to 20,000 in five years.

In 1962 Witness Lee felt led of the Lord to come to the United States, settling in California. During his 35 years of service in the U.S., he ministered in weekly meetings and weekend conferences, delivering several thousand spoken messages. Much of his speaking has since been published as over 400 titles. Many of these have been translated into over fourteen languages. He gave his last public conference in February 1997 at the age of 91.

He leaves behind a prolific presentation of the truth in the Bible. His major work, *Life-study of the Bible,* comprises over 25,000 pages of commentary on every book of the Bible from the perspective of the believers' enjoyment and experience of God's divine life in Christ through the Holy Spirit. Witness Lee was the chief editor of a new translation of the New Testament into Chinese called the Recovery Version and directed the translation of the same into English. The Recovery Version also appears in a number of other languages. He provided an extensive body of footnotes, outlines, and spiritual cross references. A radio broadcast of his messages can be heard on Christian radio stations in the United States. In 1965 Witness Lee founded Living Stream Ministry, a non-profit corporation, located in Anaheim, California, which officially presents his and Watchman Nee's ministry.

Witness Lee's ministry emphasizes the experience of Christ as life and the practical oneness of the believers as the Body of Christ. Stressing the importance of attending to both these matters, he led the churches under his care to grow in Christian life and function. He was unbending in his conviction that God's goal is not narrow sectarianism but the Body of Christ. In time, believers began to meet simply as the church in their localities in response to this conviction. In recent years a number of new churches have been raised up in Russia and in many eastern European countries.

OTHER BOOKS PUBLISHED BY
Living Stream Ministry

Titles by Witness Lee:

Abraham—Called by God	0-7363-0359-6
The Experience of Life	0-87083-417-7
The Knowledge of Life	0-87083-419-3
The Tree of Life	0-87083-300-6
The Economy of God	0-87083-415-0
The Divine Economy	0-87083-268-9
God's New Testament Economy	0-87083-199-2
The World Situation and God's Move	0-87083-092-9
Christ vs. Religion	0-87083-010-4
The All-inclusive Christ	0-87083-020-1
Gospel Outlines	0-87083-039-2
Character	0-87083-322-7
The Secret of Experiencing Christ	0-87083-227-1
The Life and Way for the Practice of the Church Life	0-87083-785-0
The Basic Revelation in the Holy Scriptures	0-87083-105-4
The Crucial Revelation of Life in the Scriptures	0-87083-372-3
The Spirit with Our Spirit	0-87083-798-2
Christ as the Reality	0-87083-047-3
The Central Line of the Divine Revelation	0-87083-960-8
The Full Knowledge of the Word of God	0-87083-289-1
Watchman Nee—A Seer of the Divine Revelation ...	0-87083-625-0

Titles by Watchman Nee:

How to Study the Bible	0-7363-0407-X
God's Overcomers	0-7363-0433-9
The New Covenant	0-7363-0088-0
The Spiritual Man 3 volumes	0-7363-0269-7
Authority and Submission	0-7363-0185-2
The Overcoming Life	1-57593-817-0
The Glorious Church	0-87083-745-1
The Prayer Ministry of the Church	0-87083-860-1
The Breaking of the Outer Man and the Release ...	1-57593-955-X
The Mystery of Christ	1-57593-954-1
The God of Abraham, Isaac, and Jacob	0-87083-932-2
The Song of Songs	0-87083-872-5
The Gospel of God 2 volumes	1-57593-953-3
The Normal Christian Church Life	0-87083-027-9
The Character of the Lord's Worker	1-57593-322-5
The Normal Christian Faith	0-87083-748-6
Watchman Nee's Testimony	0-87083-051-1

Available at
Christian bookstores, or contact Living Stream Ministry
2431 W. La Palma Ave. • Anaheim, CA 92801
1-800-549-5164 • www.livingstream.com